Reasons to be Cheerful, Part One

Toni Kent

ISBN-10: 1494340542
ISBN-13: 978-1494340544

FOREWORD

Hi, I'm Toni. Optimist, absurdist and relentlessly cheerful. Look how happy I am to be writing, and oh what big teeth I have!

The blog 'Reasons to be Cheerful' was born out of the realisation that I had, over the years, lacquered myself with more coats of corporate varnish than is normal for a person of my left-handed, right-brained, nonsensical persuasion.

I considered doing an MBA when I should have been considering how to spend more time writing. I picked up books on economics when I should have been picking flowers. At the request of various managers I tried to form opinions on virtualisation and servers that could cope with 'bursty' workloads when I really couldn't give a flying baboon in a silken cape about whether a company chooses these things or not. Little wonder that I was never a stellar sales person.

When I finally caught sight of the signs of burnout that my husband and children had seen coming for years (so much so I think our daughter's first piece of writing was in danger of being my resignation letter), I took the decision to save my sanity by leaving big business to go freelance which gave me the freedom and motivation to start a blog where I could roll around in the joy of words like a dog in a garden full of interesting smells. This is my gallop around the garden: a selection of the best bits that I hope you will enjoy and relate to. It's a celebration of how good it feels to be honest about who you are, having opinions on the really important things, acknowledging some good, good people and remembering with love those who can't be with us anymore.

And to that last point, 25% of the profits from this book will be donated to Macmillan Cancer Support (http://www.macmillan.org.uk) and a further 25% will be donated to Daisy's Dream who support children and families affected by life-threatening illness and bereavement (http://www.daisysdream.org.uk). They are good, good people and so are you. Thank you for buying this book.

CONTENTS

ACKNOWLEDGMENTS

This book is dedicated to all of the good, good people who have helped me, inspired me, made me laugh and brought great joy to my life.

Thank you to all of the people that read the blog and to those that voted for the posts to be included in this book: Becky Kent, Chris Packe, Jo McIntyre, Julie Richards, Kate Leek, Ree Chapman and Rob and Vicki Widdis. Thanks go also to all of the friends and family who allowed me to share their stories.

To Tony Cocks, thanks for the awesome cover art. The force is strong with you.

To David Stewart, thank you for your excellent proofreading services and challenging my musical references. See you on Pop Master.

To Mum, Austin, Olly, Simon, Sam and Juliet, much love. And to Dad, thanks for the blue eyes and kick-starting my love of music, I hope you are looking down and enjoying this as much as I am.

To my friends, thank you for your emotional and quite literal support when I've had too many glasses of wine. You're the best!

To my beautiful children, you are the funniest, loveliest little people I know, you make my world complete.

And to Ben. I love you mate, god only knows what I'd be without you.

1 IN THE BEGINNING

In which I chronicle my move from being a corporate monkey to a freelancer, wake up to the fact that I will have to live within my means and celebrate some rather inspiring people.

I AM NOT A SCORECARD, I AM A FREE WOMAN!

Work is an important part of my life. For 15 years, I pursued my career with vigour, moving from small tech businesses to niche vendors and then to Microsoft where I had long aspired to work.

The environment was exciting and rewarding. When it came to the birth of our two children, I enjoyed six months' maternity leave on both occasions without having to worry about the bills. On returning to work after the birth of our second child, I accepted that whilst paying two lots of nursery fees equated to a second mortgage, it was all part of the corporate experience and one day the house would be paid for and we could all pat ourselves on the back.

Then our daughter started school and the neat arrangement of having both children in the same place between 8.00am and 6.00pm was replaced with our son remaining at nursery in one village whilst our daughter attended the local school (and after-school club) from 9.00am to 5.30pm. The challenge in managing the differences in timings and locations was a something we had expected but what made it doubly difficult was that the daughter we collected at 5.30 from after school club was tired, hungry and not in the mood for telling us about her day, let alone doing homework.

I tried flexible working but discovered that instead of having a better balance, I was always 'on'. Working until 1am because I felt like I had to 'make up' for spending between 5.30pm and 8.00pm with my family (how nuts is that?!) then getting up at 6.30am, does not make for a happy or productive employee or, more importantly, parent.

I started asking myself 'what if?' questions. At work: "what if the scorecard isn't green?" and "what if I say what I really think instead what I'm supposed to say?" At home: "if I put all my energy into something I love, what could I achieve?" and "what if I could enjoy *walking* my daughter to school rather than marching, whilst constantly repeating "hurry up or we'll be late"?" My husband reminded me to make sure we addressed the "what if I don't make any money?" question, even if it did pain me to tear my mind away from the 'tra-la-la throw money at it' mentality that was a product of the lovely high salary that I was paid, towards more realistic thoughts of how much money we actually need to live on.

I sought advice and asked people within my network if they would hire me if I were a freelancer. Their responses gave me the confidence to decide that my next career move wasn't up, it was out. I wrote my resignation letter with a huge sigh of relief and have not looked back.

In the process of leaving, the network I spent 15 years building crackled into life leading me to my first contracts. It's out with meaningless meetings, scorecard metrics that I don't relate to, and working until 1am, and it's in with focusing on the work I love and recognition for delivering real value to my customers. We have more harmony in the household and I am enjoying time with the children without a device bleeping that my inbox is filling up.

Becoming a freelancer provided validation, freedom, and a chance to be the master of my own destiny. It also gave me the opportunity to see my daughter ride her bike without stabilisers for the first time – on a Wednesday afternoon…

Soundtrack: 'The Prisoner' – Iron Maiden

OH MATHEMATICS

After informing my husband that I intended to leave corporate life, he said: *"I will support your decision only if you can work out financially what it means to us."*

This was a very annoying and challenging thing for him to say to me as I used to feel a perverse sense of pride in saying, "I'm not good at maths", or, even worse, "I don't *do* maths." It was a smart move on his part, as years of receiving a generous salary and benefits package had effectively divorced my brain from understanding the actual cost of things and the value of money.

So, I did as I was told, developed best and worst case scenarios, and so far, so good. However, what is interesting to me looking back is that my thought process was "How much do I need to earn to keep the lifestyle that I enjoy?"

In the past 18 months that thinking has shifted to can I have a lifestyle that I enjoy that isn't centred on earning money?"

A good example of this is the car I used to drive. Bought on a finance plan when in possession of a car allowance I chose the most highly-specced thing I could find. Forget servicing/tyres/tax - the allowance all went on added extras such as satnav and heated seats (as if my backside doesn't do a good enough job of keeping itself warm!). Then a couple of months ago as I did my year end accounts I thought it would be a good time to look at our overall financial health and calculated how much I would need to earn before tax to cover the finance repayments. I nearly fell over. Finally the penny dropped that I was working my (very warm) backside off to pay for a car that was only being driven two or three days a week and hardly ever with more than two people in it...I gave myself a slap around the face and a 'D-minus' with a big red pen.

So the car went, swapped for a much cheaper, older model. It doesn't have satnav, parking sensors or leather seats but I can read a map (ok, I can't - I get the directions from the AA website and write them down on the back of an envelope which then gets stuck to the dashboard), park using my mirrors and if I'm that desperate for the feel of leather, then I'll have to make like a Hairy Biker and buy a nice pair of trousers.

The sense of freedom from having that financial weight lifted is fantastic - now my wages can go on the important things such as the mortgage, the children's shoes, and wine!

Soundtrack: 'Mathematics' – Cherry Ghost

CAN YOU SEE THE REAL ME?

"Hey, I really like your tattoos."

I said this to the guy on the till in H&M. They were a bit old school in topic (ships, birds, mermaids) but really beautifully done and, as he could see I was staring at them, it would have been terrible manners not to explain why.

With the inking, an ear stretcher and facial piercings he was giving a very visible statement about who he is and in a way that would be difficult to conceal unless he took to wearing a boiler suit and a balaclava.

This led to a conversation one Friday night some about how much we are our 'true' selves at work, which leads me to this piece...

When I worked for a corporate business I concealed parts of my character in the belief that it would help me to be more successful. I thought that you needed to act in a certain way and took to emulating the traits of people I perceived to be successful in the hope it would help to further my career. This meant toning down my sense of the absurd and hiding the emotional side of my personality - basically I stopped having, and being, fun.

Not surprisingly, it didn't take long to get found out and there were a couple of instances where I learned that forcing yourself to fit an ideal that is very different to who you are is never going to work. During an office move I tripped over a packing crate and hurt my leg so badly that it made me cry (justified: there was blood and everything). Whilst apologising to a colleague who had helped me up for crying in front of her, she said, "Don't be silly, it just shows that you're human." Had I not appeared human up until then?

The second incident was when I was a manager, and I asked a member of the team why she was so emotional about a change in the business. Her response was, "What would you know? You're like a robot!" I was shocked by her opinion but, in hindsight, she wasn't far off the mark. Unfortunately, what I hid at work would come out at home where I would end up in hysterics for the smallest thing such as dropping a plate or stubbing my toe. I realised this was not a healthy place to be.

At that point I made some changes and became an account manager where I worked with external businesses rather than focusing on internal tasks. There is nothing like spending time with people who have run their own company for 25 years and know more than a thing or two about life to help you get over yourself and realise that life in the real world is very different to that in the ivory tower.

Their input (and saying things like, "Toni, you're still a bit of a robot.") set me on a path to being more honest with myself and others about who I am. The most interesting thing I discovered was the more I am myself, the more I enjoy myself, and the more I enjoy myself, the more successful I am at work (and at home too!). The children couldn't give a monkey's about my knowledge of scorecarding, running a 'Quarterly Business Review' and 'IT Transformation' but they do love my passion for music, art and language, and my ability to impersonate the Cookie Monster and Yoda (but not at the same time).

Of course this does not mean that I am no longer professional or courteous at work, and I don't turn up with a thong sticking up out of the back of my trousers, but now that I work for myself I am committed to embracing even more of what makes me who I am, and I will kick my own arse if I don't stick to it!

Soundtrack: 'The Real Me' – The Who

ALL YOU GOOD, GOOD PEOPLE

If I hear one more person moan about something not working out for them because it was someone else's fault then I will scream.

Life is short, challenging, difficult, frustrating, upsetting and frightening at times. But it can also be joyous, magical, incredible, breath-taking and brilliant.

It is so easy to be distracted by stories about people who have done terrible things to others, who prey on the vulnerable and seek to gain satisfaction by upsetting others. What this sometimes makes us forget is that, generally, people are good.

Throughout my life I have met people who are inspirational, uplifting, kind and generous. Some standouts for me are:

– The school friends who linked arms with me when we each lost a parent, making sure we made it out of our teenage years in one piece.

– The NCT teacher who made the mothers in our group feel empowered, and scared the living daylights out of the fathers with her videos and graphic descriptions of the 'wonder' that is childbirth.

– The sales director who takes time out from being responsible for a multimillion pound business to share his experiences and help me figure out what I'm going to do next in return for a pint.

- The nurse who hugged me in comfort and friendship after the difficult birth of my son.

- The friends with whom I have laughed until my cheeks are sore and danced until my feet ache.

- Whoever it was that paid for the bar at our wedding - still a secret after all these years!

- The neighbours who have loaned lawnmowers, dug my car out of the drive (note to self: rear-wheel drive and deep gravel do not mix), babysat, collected in-laws lost in the rain and generally been brilliant.

- My children who have filled my life with light and laughter and taught me to be able to deal with explosions from any orifice during a meal without breaking a sweat.

- My husband. He is a lucky boy but I know I am bloody hard work at times.

So here's to all the good, good people that I've met out there and to all the ones to come.

Soundtrack: 'All You Good Good People' - Embrace

2 SOMETIMES IT'S HARD TO BE A WOMAN

Sometimes it's hard to be a man too but there's not a lot I can tell you about that. Instead, here's my take on hair removal, domestic slovenliness, face origami and kitchen fires. That last one is all Jamie Oliver's fault.

HOW DOES YOUR GARDEN GROW?

What is it with women and hair? We enter the world with a little on our heads (or an amazing amount if you're my friend's daughter who looked like Elvis' lovechild when she was born) and then, in the same way that boys do, just 'have hair' until we hit puberty. At that point it becomes a *massive* issue. Whether it's on your head, under your arms, or in your knickers, you absolutely must control it!

Becoming a teenager in the late '80s, my memories of this are as follows:

- Backcombing, bleaching and generally ruining the hair on my head.

- Being told by older friends that having hairy legs is 'rank' and then carving a strip of skin off each shinbone after applying my dad's guardless razor to them like you would a vegetable peeler to a carrot.

- Unwisely deciding with a friend to shave our forearms because they were 'well hairy'. We did. It grew back thicker.

Then as early adulthood arrived, managing your bikini line became important thanks to the 'tanga' brief and amazingly high-cut swimming costumes (thanks a lot Baywatch!). This led to various experiments with epilators (ouch!), waxing (Jesus that hurts!), and hair removal cream (oh the stench!) before going back to razors with which, by now, I had managed to avoid mutilating myself with.

And so it carries on into adulthood: an ever-present need to control the hair that nature has blessed/cursed you with. To date this has just been part of the female experience for me:

women groom and men do whatever they can be arsed to do.

It had never crossed my mind that at some point I might need to explain the ridiculous set-up that is female hair maintenance until my daughter asked me, "Mummy, why is there so much hair coming out of that lady's swimming costume?"

Growing up in a time when there was not an obsession with reducing your pubic hair to a 'landing strip' or removing it entirely meant I never had to have a conversation about that area of grooming with my own mother. Apart from leg-shaving (even when I was little, black leg hairs showing through American Tan tights was a no-no), people just had body hair and that was it.

Interestingly, the children's only concern when it comes to men and hair is whether the gentleman has a 'baldy head' or not. Body-wise he could have it growing like lichen from his shoulders to his ankles, exploding from ears and nasal passages, and carry enormous 'welcome mats' on his chest and back and they wouldn't bat an eyelid.

So what was my response? Well, after ushering my daughter out of the changing room and hoping she had not been overheard, I said "there just is." I realised that for now, that would have to do. I'm not ready to introduce the concept of women thinking they have to alter their appearance in that regard and in the meantime will just have to hope that we don't bump into the woman so blessed in the lady-garden department again anytime soon.

Soundtrack: 'Mary, Mary, Quite Contrary' – 18th Century English Nursery Rhyme

WILL YOU RECOGNISE ME?

How often do you get a 'thank you' for doing the hoovering? The washing? Changing the beds?

A friend of mine refers to these domestic tasks as the 'silent' jobs. The boring, necessary stuff that has to happen to make a household run but for which you rarely get a 'thank you'. In most instances it doesn't matter and expecting a round of applause for cleaning the barbecue is taking it a bit far. But how about for doing the lion's share of bringing up the children? Surely that's worthy of major recognition?

At work, unless you have a particularly disengaged boss, or your customers are never happy, you're likely to be thanked or rewarded on a fairly regular basis (see 'Paid in Full' for more on that topic). If you've made (or are planning to make) the switch from working full-time to being at home with the children full-time then this is a significant change and one to which I hadn't given any thought before going on my first period of maternity leave.

Going from an environment where you are encouraged to pursue plaudits and are paid based on your performance, to one where you do something that is arguably more significant but receives less overt recognition is very difficult and wasn't something that was mentioned during the ante-natal classes that I attended. I think it should have been.

It is viewed as the 'right thing to do' to see parents as entirely equal in the upbringing of their children but it would be fairer (and more accurate) to say that the one who stays at home / is at home more, should be given greater credit. It is a brave man or woman who says to their wife or husband that they have had more influence on the development of their children, but you would never get such daintiness were it two colleagues discussing who had contributed more to a particular project.

Someone who got it right is a very enlightened friend of mine, Nicky. She saw this coming as she left a successful sales job to have her daughter, and planned to take at least a year off. She explained to her husband that if he wanted a happy wife, then he needed to make sure he recognised her efforts and achievements, and acknowledged that what she did was just as valid as him dedicating his day to generating the household income. The net result was, as well experiencing the joy that comes with being so involved in your child's early years, she also received acknowledgement and reassurance from the person that she loves.

I thought this was such a smart thing to do, and not something that should be restricted to people that are leaving, or putting on hold, a big career. I think it should be discussed amongst all parents and potential parents. Our children don't morph into the fantastical people that they become on their own, so why aren't we patting ourselves on the back more often?

Soundtrack: 'Don't You (Forget About Me)' - Simple Minds

DANCE LITTLE SISTER

I have a little sister. Well when I say 'little', she's 18 years younger than I am. Which makes her little. To me.

Having a sister so much younger than me is not only a great way to keep vaguely connected with current fashion trends (most of which I wore twenty years ago - tribal prints anyone?) and music (I can't go there without sounding like my mum) but it also makes me consider what I might have wished I had known before embarking on some of my more 'interesting' teenage adventures.

Of course, my sister does not wish for me to give her advice because that would be, 'like, majorly embarrassing'. So, instead, here are the things my teenage self would tell her, from one 19-year-old to another (with just a little hindsight thrown in...).

1. Dance, dance, and dance some more! Go to clubs, gigs, festivals and house parties. Throw yourself about with abandon and enjoy the agony that is your feet hurting from three hours on the dance floor. Get dizzy in the moshpit: it will leave you beer-soaked and exhausted but it is exhilarating.

2. Be your own person. Trust your instincts and do what makes you happy, no one knows you better than you do, don't let other people make your decisions. Be it on boys, what dress to wear or whether Dappy would win in a fight against Plan B - make the choice your own.

3. Don't dumb down your life. Is Kerry Katona's 'new body' really important to you? Fancy spending your days watching people arguing about the paternity of their children? I didn't think so. Stop watching Jeremy Kyle and

reading Heat magazine *immediately*.

4. Dream big. Make your ambitions massive ones, they will inspire you to achieve more. That said, I did start out my first half marathon thinking "what if I *won* it?" Now, that's just bloody ridiculous. Of course I was never going to win, but it did give me the boost I needed to get to the end, after which I felt elated, then crippled and sick, and I cried because I couldn't find my husband. Sometimes getting what you want feels weird, but that's not a reason not to do it - go after the big stuff!

5. Wear a bikini. That flat stomach of yours is amazing, it won't look like that once your children have finished with it.

So that's it. I'm sure there's more, but my 19-year-old self is busy figuring out how she's going to get to a house party that's ten miles away when she can't drive and has no money for a taxi...

Soundtrack: 'Dance Little Sister' – Terence Trent D'Arby

PS: Since this post was originally written my sister wishes it to be known that she doesn't watch Jeremy Kyle or read Heat. And that she thinks Plan B would most certainly beat Dappy!

I GET SO EMOTIONAL

I took the children to see *The Croods* at the cinema. It's a visual spectacular with a plot that involves a cave-family realising that they have must change or die because 'the end is coming'. Volcanoes erupt, the land parts, mountains shake and their cave is decimated. We crunch through popcorn and I am wistful for the days of my youth where going to the cinema was about queuing outside the ABC in a state of near hysteria at getting to see *the latest film* but I am grateful that the seats today are massive and nobody smokes or throws Mint Imperials at the back of your head.

And then towards the end of the film, 'Mr Crood' is separated from his family and his daughter starts crying, and so do I. For goodness sake! I am crying at a children's film. Not heaving sobs of heartache you must understand, but more than a couple of tears slide their way down my face at the sight of the cave girl's massive tear-filled eyes and trembling bottom lip. This was not a one off either. Since having children there aren't many programmes, songs or news stories that don't set me off. That's why mums always have a tissue up their sleeve, not for bogey-noses, but in case a baby smiles at them or a dog whimpers or a song that contains a tinkly piano comes on the radio.

You might think that I shouldn't be so emotional but it appears to be programmed into me. From having a parent's-eye view of 'terrible twos' and wild boys, to remembering my own teenage angst (and really, really hoping that my children somehow magically skip that) to the wonder of reproductive hormones, I'm inclined to believe we're designed to be emotional from the minute we shout our way indignantly into the world. Having children aside, there has been enough happen in my life over the years to make me shed a tear or two and when it feels like it has all got too much, I am thankful to have found my 'fix': running. Magical stuff.

And then one day I'm talking to a friend who utters the word 'peri-menopausal'. I'm wondering if this is a new type of Nando's flavour but no, she tells me it is the time before you are 'pre-menopausal'. I think the lifespan of a man is generally taken to be as Morrissey so succinctly puts it in 'Cemetry Gates': "they were born and then they lived and then they died." I'm not sure quite why women's lives are sliced into ever tinier sections to be labelled and treated. The cynic in me says it's because the drug companies would like to find new reasons to sell us gallons of evening primrose and anti-ageing pills when we all know that a glass of wine and good company has a significantly greater impact on your mood. Or maybe they are really run by mega-hippies that want to help us all chill out as we reach middle age.

The answer may not materialise to me for quite some time, so until the point that I am peri, piri, pingy, poingy or whatever it is that I am to be labelled, I shall carry on crying at kids' films, and, if all the terrible things that my friend described really are on the way, I'm going to need a new pair of running shoes.

Soundtrack: 'So Emotional' – Whitney Houston

ABSOLUTELY FLAWLESS

Here are some things that, to the best of my knowledge, the skin around my eyes has not been responsible for:

Passing my driving test

Securing our mortgage

Prompting my move from employee to freelancer

Our decision to get married

Brilliant moments with lifelong friends

I know this, but spend a disproportionate amount of time thinking about what I can do to reduce the appearance of the 'sunburst' that emanates from around my eyes and is somewhat disturbingly working its way outwards until it reaches my hairline or falls off the edge of my jaw.

Given the amount that I smile and the extent to which these lines appear throughout my family, this is a ridiculous thought: I am genetically predisposed to have them. It's not going to get any better either so why the hell am I worrying about it now? Perhaps instead I should be looking forward to the fun I'll be able to have in 30 years' time when I will be able to use origami techniques to fold my face into new and interesting shapes!

It is a vain and fruitless worry and yet so many smart women are equally concerned with their breasts, legs, bottoms, necks, hands... We are too wobbly, wrinkly, not brown enough or pouty enough to make it in today's world and don't get me started on hair. Why else would such a massive beauty industry exist without these insecurities and what on earth are they going to focus on next? Our elbows?

Don't get me wrong, I love wearing make-up and being pampered at the spa, but ads that focus on 'turning back the clock' or preventing the march of nature on a woman's body unsettle me. These help reinforce the view that women must not appear older than 25 and if your body changes after having children you have 'failed'. So we spend more time and money per ounce on these products than we would on gold chasing a version of perfection that can't be achieved. Brilliant, clever women worrying about something that is not within their power to change unless they're up for a lifetime of tweaks, nips and tucks until they finally give in to the realisation that no surgery or technology is going to make them look convincingly the same as a dewy-skinned teenager.

The weird thing is that we do this to ourselves but generally not to those that we care about. When was the last time you didn't accept a phone call from a friend on the basis that one of her boobs is a bit bigger than the other or she can no longer balance a tea tray on her booty? We see the people we love for who they are: their achievements and idiosyncrasies, the things that delight us about them and those that make them bloody annoying. We engage with them on the basis of their minds and spirit, not how physically 'flawless' they are.

Soundtrack: 'Flawless' – The Ones

BECAUSE YOU'RE GORGEOUS

It is about time that L'Oréal gave up on 'Because You're Worth It'. Memorable strapline that it is, I do find it just the tiniest bit patronising. For that reason, I would like to offer up an alternative to the L'Oréal view that all women want is glossy tresses and 'Volume Million' (what?!) eyelashes - even if they are rather nice.

This thought was prompted by the fantastic lunch that I had with a friend yesterday. She is fun and feisty, a lady that can count photographer, film crew member, financial controller, horse rider, graduate, artist and boxer amongst her many talents. To that I would add adventuress, raconteur and mentor, someone with whom I could happily discuss anything from libraries to libido. She also happens to be just over ten years older than me but she is all of the above before the number that is her age. As it goes, our conversation covered our own experiences as women, the right for girls to be properly educated, how to make sure you are paid what you are worth, and for women to have (and expect) boardroom and bedroom equality.

My friend is a strong, inspirational woman and someone with whom I am excited to have made a connection as this could not have come at a better time for me. I careered through my teenage years in a haze of cheap alcohol, dedicated my twenties and early thirties to pursuing a career with gusto whilst building a family and now, in my late thirties, I am reaching for financial freedom and using my talents and abilities to benefit those around me in a more meaningful way. You can try to do these things on your own but it works so much better if you have a great coach. Where would Daniel-san have been without Mr Miyagi? Billy Elliot without Mrs Wilkinson? Rocky Balboa without Mickey Goldmill? We need these people in our lives and we need to be them to other people on the way up.

I think that there are a lot of women of my generation who are seeking this kind of coaching relationship. I know plenty of women who feel they are pigeon-holed because they work. Women who struggle to find other women to talk to about their ambitions, who feel 'shut-out' by colleagues or other parents on the playground because they think they are being judged for being too career-focused or family-focused. If you are a woman that wants to spend more time with your family but still earn a decent living finding someone to guide you and take you seriously can be even harder. It is fascinating to observe the difference in reactions from people when you say you are 'part-time' versus 'self-employed', or working 'flexi-hours' versus being a 'freelancer'.

Depending on what environment you were last in, or are still in, it can seem hard to get to know a woman who has achieved the things that you are seeking and could give you good advice on how to get there. Don't feel too shy to ask a woman you admire for her help; without exception I have found that successful women will offer some of their time to help another woman find her version of success. If you don't feel you have the opportunity to meet other women in your workplace or where you live, make the time to meet. Find any excuse - coffee, book club, play date, night on the tiles - whatever it is you choose to do, bring people together.

We had a pub-based gathering recently of women in our village based around the fact that we all have children at school. It only took a little bit of talking to get past the stuff about the kids and onto the real things - what people really want to do and what's frustrating them at work or at home. This brought about some great conversations about what we might be able to offer to one another. There was a rich pool of interesting and talented women, right there, and some connections were made meaning that we can help each other out, outside of the school run. That's if we can remember all the things we spoke about...there was a lot of wine being drunk!

This focus on women helping one another is not to say that I am anti-men. Completely the opposite, I am a big believer when it comes to our menfolk, I am a 'man fan' if you like, but I do think that there is a lack of support for us ladies, from us ladies. It needs to start with us. We have to make sure we're helping each other and I am grateful to have found some inspirational women who have helped me so far, and some who will help me navigate the next chapter in my life. As Madeleine Albright (the first woman to become United States Secretary of State) said in a keynote speech she delivered in 2006: "There is a special place in hell for women who don't help other women."

So L'Oréal, with your lovely, shiny-haired ladies, whilst it's wonderful that you're making Cheryl Cole very rich by paying her enormous amounts of money to tell us that we're worth the £6.49 that it costs for your hair dye, what we actually want doesn't come from your factories: we women are worth one hell of a lot more.

PS: Whilst you're summoning up the courage to speak to the female VP of Sales or the time to arrange a drinks night, you might be interested in the following:

http://www.careersadviceforambitiouswomen.com/ - A brilliant, practical, guide to combining motherhood with a fulfilling career, written by a woman who has done just that. It also has the best closing line of any book I have ever read. Thank you Mrs Moneypenny!

http://www.caitlinmoran.co.uk/index.php - Reading 'How to be a Woman' gave me the kick up the arse I needed to get writing properly.

http://blogs.forbes.com/jessicahagy/ - Jessica Hagy manages to combine words and pictures to inspirational effect.

Soundtrack: *'You're Gorgeous' - Babybird*

RAGE AGAINST THE (WASHING) MACHINE

There is a conspiracy happening within my house. Led by my husband's quest for perfection in all things technical, things that were once simple have become increasingly complex.

Our lovely little camera that we bought six years ago to document our first days as parents has been replaced by a Digital SLR monstrosity. So large it requires its own handbag, so complicated the instruction book could prop up a wonky table, so expensive it cannot be taken to the beach for fear that sand will get into it. This camera was once cradled and cooed over, but it now stays in a cupboard, gets an airing on birthdays and at Christmas and everything else is snapped by my (easy-to-use, portable, light, seaside-proof) phone.

The lawnmower is gigantic, petrol-powered, and requires Popeye to pull the ripcord. On the occasions where I have tried to use it I have been hauled up the garden like a three-year-old trying to walk a whippet that's just seen a rabbit. It is a man's machine and I am not Hulk Hogan. Complain away husband that I do not mow the lawn, or buy me a Flymo and I will happily oblige.

There are other things: the thermostats for the three different heating systems we have, the hi-fi (do people still use that term?) in our bedroom with an alarm clock that I am unable to programme, and the television control that has buttons that mean nothing to me. I am afraid to be left in the house on my own in the winter, for fear of contracting hypothermia and no one being able to reach me because the lawn will have reclaimed the path and grown taller than the front door.

So when it came to replacing the washing machine there was no way that decision wasn't going to be mine.

The new addition to our kitchen is simple, elegant and does exactly what I need it to do. And whilst I might perish because I couldn't work the oven or heat the house, when the paramedics finally cut their way to the front door with a scythe, they will find me in pristine knickers!

OLIVER'S ARMY

Oh Jamie Oliver, with your winning smile, infectious enthusiasm and genuine commitment to changing the relationship that people have with food. You make us thoughtful, inspire us to want better nutrition for our families, and challenge our largest institutions to do better by our children. You also made me set fire to my kitchen.

I am not a natural cook, but neither am I a 'microwave mealer'. My repertoire (if you were to call it that) includes a mean lasagne, spaghetti bolognese, cottage pie and if there is no mince to be had, I can cook a rather lovely roast chicken. But that's pretty much it and, because of that, almost all of the cooking in our house falls to my husband who reads the Leith Cookery Bible for fun and who must be some kind of sorcerer for he magics up fine meals witho ut swearing, shouting at inanimate objects, or injuring himself.

There are times when I feel that I should make more of an effort, and during one such period I dusted off the *Jamie's 30-Minute Meals* cookery book to learn to start rustling up some more exciting meals than my usual 'mince wonder'. Some of the dishes, like the 'Tasty Crusted Cod' on page 140 were rather good, delicious even, but they required me to have "absolute silence!" in the kitchen and created an hour's worth of washing up.

What was somewhat less successful was the 'Cheat's Pizza'. Apparently I was supposed to be able to create one pizza, three 'delish' salads and a squashed cherries and vanilla cream dessert all within half an hour. Based on my previous experience I thought I'd go just for the pizza and set all of my ingredients out. At the appropriate point, I followed the instructions to put the frying pan on a high heat whilst putting the dough ingredients into a food processor, whizzing them up, taking the dough out and rolling it flat. By Jamie's calculations I think this should have taken less than a minute. It is entirely possible that in 'Toni time' this equated to five or six minutes and so when I 'drizzled some olive oil' into the pan I was met with a sheet of flame.

For a moment I stood there looking at it, and somewhere in the back of my mind I felt compelled to start dancing in homage to *Tales of the Unexpected* but then realised that if I didn't extinguish the fire quickly, it would set off the smoke alarm, wake the children and quite possibly set the entire kitchen alight. I can cope with a kitchen on fire but not children that have been startled out of their slumber, so I gathered my wits about me, fetched a wet tea towel and took the smoking pan into the garden where it would prove less of a danger to my family.

After eating a sandwich for my supper because bread = no fire, I brought the pan in, scrubbed it and got rid of most of the damage. The pan still bears a black crescent that mocks me every time I fry some garlic and onions (again) to make the base for my lasagne sauce (again). I am hopeful that this will fade over time but until then it keeps me on the straight and mince-based narrow.

This experience has taught me that if you are a cook or a chef then yes, 30 minutes is entirely doable to create a satisfying and nutritious meal but if you are an easily distracted person who has a whole list of other things you'd rather be doing than cooking, it is not such an easy task. So from now on I'll be sticking to what I know, and taking the *Jamie's 15-Minute Meals* book off my Christmas list...mince for tea again, kids?

Soundtrack: 'Oliver's Army' - Elvis Costello

3 FASHION

Ah fashion I love you and hate you in equal measure. You bring me evening gowns, heels and beautiful handbags and then you go and spoil it all with Spanx.

LITTLE GREEN (DUSTBIN) BAG

I have recently been introduced to a shopping site called 'Bag Servant' (www.bagservant.co.uk) and what a delicious (and potentially dangerous) place it is to spend a lunch hour. From Biba to Balenciaga and Radley to Ralph Lauren it's got the lot, and, best of all, you can try them on thanks to a neat bit of technology. I am thoroughly enjoying mentally spending money on all sorts of goodies even though I know I can only afford the sale stock.

And it's a good thing that I can't afford the high-end candy because my own relationship with handbags goes thus:

I buy one and promise faithfully that I will *not let this one turn into a portable dustbin.* I momentarily covet and care for it and then I end up putting it down in some kind of puddle in the playground / at soft play (see 'What a Girl Wants' for more on that) thereby spoiling the leather and breaking the seal on keeping my bag well cared for.

The last bag this happened to is (what was) a very lovely butter-soft purple leather tote with silky cream lining that smelled like heaven and appeared to answer my need for a bag that would carry my laptop but still look great. The first thing I did was overstuff it when trying to take everything as carry-on for a business trip which resulted in a rivet popping off and one of the tags breaking. I then put it on the (what was bound to be dirty) floor of a school hall whilst the children were at a trampolining lesson, and failed to spot the orange juice that was just waiting for someone (me) to plant their bag or foot in it. The warm sticky liquid added a nice dark patch to the bottom of the bag, another 'battle scar' to take my bag from coveted to careworn. That's the outside trashed then. But what of the inside?

Well, I was hoping it might be as organised as the *My Mummy's Bag* book that I recently bought which is full of lovely pull-out cardboard pieces that reflect what a working mother might have in her handbag (laptop, hanky, keys, mobile, picture of the children, lists of things to do, lipstick, and in a nice touch, a leopard-print shoe just like the ones I have). I bought the book for my daughter as I thought it vaguely reflected what my day is like and she enjoys pretending to go off to work. But I know the truth, my bag is nothing like that example of organised womanhood. Here's what is actually in it:

A wallet stuffed with receipts, cards, photos of the children and - in a rare state of affairs - some money!

Boots Double Points vouchers that I will never use on mascara because they all get spent on Calpol.

A Debenhams Beauty Club statement which has £3.29 on it because my shopping there is now restricted to children's pants and pyjamas.

An old-school multi-coloured biro. Red, green, blue and black all in one pen!

My old phone, because I can't be arsed to find a proper place for it / put it in the recycling pot.

Free crayons from the restaurant at Camp Hopson of Newbury - one of two reasons the children love going there. The other is it has an old-fashioned fundraising box in the shape of a three-feet tall bear. God knows how old it is but I hope they don't plan to remove it or I'll end up having to buy it off them.

One giant 'flump' which did not make it back into the bag.

A little bit of Clarins, darling (I do make an effort sometimes)

One long orange balloon

A mouse. For a computer. Although from the hole in one of the inside pockets it is possible that a live mouse has been in there. Perhaps it was after the unidentifiable crumbs in the very bottom - don't say that you haven't got any lurking in the bottom of your bag!

It didn't contain my keys. I never know where they are, it is my morning sport to try and find them.

I tipped the bag out, catalogued the contents, and (giant flump aside) put it all back in. It is a portable dustbin once again. I know I should be sorting, decanting, organising and throwing away but despite my best efforts the detritus of everyday life seems to flow back into the bag within the space of a week. So I'm going to use this as a public forum to ask Bag Servant to add a new service: one that turns your portable dustbin back into a beautiful bag. No? Oh well, I'll just have to find myself a new one but this time I *promise* to look after it!

Soundtrack: 'Little Green Bag' - George Baker

ITSY BITSY TEENY WEENY

Sunday is 'Family Swim Day' in our house and so this weekend we undertook the familiar routine of scraping back hair, putting on sloppy clothes and travelling to the local pool.

Having had two children my bikini years are long gone but I found its bigger sister; the 'Tankini', a more forgiving item of swimwear offering good coverage whilst suggesting that I still take a degree of interest in my appearance.

Unfortunately the tankini in my bag was meant more for lounging poolside than swimming and my careless habit of slinging it in the wash with everything else meant it had finally given up the ghost - the bottoms would hold up no more. With no desire to reveal my grooming habits to the entire pool and two children threatening disobedience on an apocalyptic scale if they could not have their weekly splashabout, I knew I would have to buy my way out of the situation.

Rail after rail of Zoggs and Speedo swimwear decorated the walls at the pool's shop. Sensible, racer-back, full-coverage items in dark colours with the occasional neon line thrown in for fun. This was not a place for trends, it was for proper swimmers, who can do a decent front crawl without filling their nasal passages with chlorine and other people's wee.

After a short period of trying things on in the disabled toilet, which the children informed me 'smelled of old people', I made my selection and headed into the pool. And was instantly converted.

For years I had struggled to avoid things riding up, riding down, spilling out, or being exposed by the children as they half-drowned me by hanging onto any body part they could reach. Suddenly I was able to join in properly, get knocked about by the wave machine and go down the slide with everything staying in its rightful place.

So hurrah for my first 'proper' swimsuit - you might not be sexy but I sure as hell love you!

PS: I shall make it my life's work to ensure this attitude does not extend to my shoes. As long as I have feet the heels stay!

Soundtrack: 'Itsy Bitsy Teeny Weeny Yellow Polka Dot Bikini' – Brian Hyland

HANDBAGS AND GLADRAGS

This post is coming to you from a caravan park in Poole and oh how the humble 'van' has changed. Rather than a site for tow-alongs and tents for proper camping, this is acres of mobile homes centred around an entertainment complex, pool and spa.

We are here thanks to the kindness of relatives allowing us to use their 'Monaco Super' (nothing Monaco about it, but I'll give it the 'super') to continue our summer holiday quest of trying fruitlessly to get the children to do as we've asked them, but in a seaside setting. As the park has a mix of holidaymakers, from those renting a mobile home by the sea for a week to those that have paid anything up to £150,000 to buy one, there is a wide variety of families staying here which means great people watching opportunities.

One of these opportunities is the nightly show featuring holiday reps dressed as low-budget fictional characters, loud music and flashing lights which, combined with the gallons of Capri-Sun on offer, whips the children into a frenzy. They love it of course and, after a day at the seaside which is scientifically proven not to be relaxing if it includes children under the age of five, we are too tired to do anything but give in.

So we settle down with a glass of something cold, the kids have fun, and whilst the entertainment is pretty good, the best part is coming home. The reason for this is that by 8pm, when we're on our way back, we pass a lot of families who are just beginning their evenings and in quite some style.

Over the past few nights I have seen more glamorous

women, and men in sharply-ironed shirts and shiny shoes than I thought possible. Given that my holiday wardrobe is a cross between the Ramones and All Saints (think skinny jeans, combats, vest-tops and washed-out t-shirts) I knew I was going to be short on 'going out' clothes but nothing had prepared me for the lady in a lycra and chiffon dress with five-inch stillettos that I saw leading her brood for a family night out. She had pushed a twin buggy half a mile uphill whilst Dad escorted a further two equally well turned out children and there was neither a hair nor heel out of place. Impressive.

As well as that particular family there have been glossy tresses, Mulberry handbags (including one on Swanage beach being used as *a beach bag!*), plunging fronts, open backs, skirts slashed to the thigh, leopard print, sequins, neon and body-con, and an abundance of 'mini-me' children. By contrast, we resembled Victorian orphans and whilst for a moment it caused me to reconsider my future packing to include couture and curling tongs, the fact is that I really can't be bothered. Living in a rural village, and going primarily on beach and farm holidays results in dresses and heels being reserved for rare nights in town à deux or girlie nights where our mere presence as mums that don't get out much frightens everyone else off the dance floor.

I enjoy the spectacle of other people's big nights out as they remind me of my own childhood trips "dahn the Welly" (the Wellington Social Club, no less) where, on Friday and Saturday nights, it was The Law to dress your best. It may well be that we only went there a handful of times but the memory of the whole family getting properly dressed up is a powerful one. We had a photo taken before one such outing which features me wearing green velvet pedal pushers with matching waistcoat, and a blouse with a pussycat-bow. Sounds a bit Peter Pan meets Margaret Thatcher today, but for the early '80s I was one cool eight-year-old.

Those were very happy times indeed but reflecting on them has reminded me that my job is not to try to recreate my childhood for our children - what they choose to remember and hold as their memories will be up to them. Instead, I shall celebrate others' sequins, marvel at their manicures and await with interest next year's visit to find out what it is I should be wearing - if I could only tear myself away from my skinny jeans.......

Soundtrack: 'Handbags and Gladrags' – Rod Stewart

SPANX FOR THE MEMORIES

I have bought my first piece of control underwear. The forthcoming wedding of our friends necessitates the wearing of a dress, and its fine jersey fabric delivers a damning verdict on my behind.

If I were a man, I would think to myself "this doesn't look right so I won't buy it." Not me: the dress is perfect, it's my body that needs changing. So now I have this tube of nude-coloured fabric that is distantly related to the black lycra skirts that my friends and I used to wear as 18-year-olds, but it is definitely not to be worn as outerwear (unless things get very silly at the reception).

As with most things I am late to this game. Long before 'Bridget Jones' I witnessed a friend putting on control knickers over control shorts so she could wear her size 10 trousers again after having her second child.

Another friend recently told me that she is going to have "She lived and died in Spanx" etched on her gravestone...now there's a brand ambassador!

Underneath his clothes, my husband will wear normal underwear like normal people do - no blood flow restricting, horribly coloured, surprisingly expensive compression bandage for him: just a nice comfy pair of boxers. Oh how I will envy him come the end of the night.

In writing this piece I see what madness this is but I will not be beaten by a dress! And if you happen to be at the same wedding as me and you see me listing in a corner, it won't be because I've had a drink too many (although I will have tried my very best to do so), it will be because I have fainted - Victorian style.

WHAT A GIRL WANTS, WHAT A GIRL NEEDS

Whilst browsing a website that I quite like for fashion tip-offs, (www.avenue57.com), I came across Easy Living magazine's 'School Runway' – a page where mums can upload photos of themselves in outfits that they wear for the school run in order to look like they sail through motherhood without a hair out of place - and I was amazed. Whilst a few of the women were wearing normal clothes, most of the women were wearing proper 'outfits', complete with statement handbags, improbable heels and designer cloaks, jumpsuits, and corsets. I am willing to bet that they had dressed up especially and made their nannies hide out of shot because I'm not buying that these are normal pictures. Mild irritation aside that these ladies looked impossibly glamorous at 8am, and that I have a far more limited budget than them, my argument is this:

When you do the school run, unless you are driving, or even better, you have a chauffeur, it is simply not possible to do it in the kind of clothes that you wear in your imagination. I would love to spend my days wearing beautifully-tailored trousers, gossamer-fine knitwear and chic shoes. In the summer this would be swapped for flirty tea dresses, strappy sandals and some Jackie-O sunglasses, and if I really wanted to go to town, perhaps I would wear a dramatic gown and stunning heels and tip up sipping a cocktail. But no, this would not work because what you actually need is the following:

A hood. Because it will in all likelihood rain whilst you are walking to / from school and it is not possible to carry an umbrella and try to stay in control of two six-year-olds who would like you to carry their PE kits, lunch boxes and book bags while they pretend to be horses.

Flat shoes. If at some point you need to run away from the rain / after a child / to school because you're late (again), you will fare better in flats. As a lifelong lover of heels I have compromised with cowboy boots but it still feels like a betrayal.

Massive pockets or a bag that it's ok to get trashed. Even if you don't carry much in the way of stuff, your child will be guaranteed to give you at least one thing to take care of as soon as they reach you in the school playground. It will probably be wet, or sticky, or chewed, or all three. Chuck it in your handbag and pray it doesn't stick to your phone. And if you go to the park on the way home then you must be prepared to leave your bag on wet grass or some unspecified goo that you didn't see when putting it down to push your child on the swing. Pray that it is Diet Coke and not wee.

There are some mums who carry the above off really well, teaming a retro parka with skinny jeans and biker boots or who are still young enough to look indie with a tour t-shirt, a pair of black drainpipes and battered Converse. For me though, there are times when I get back after dropping my daughter off and think "what the hell have I just left the house in?" As it is often a combination of skinny combat trousers, the aforementioned cowboy boots, an ancient hoody, and a quilted jacket (with a hood - let's not forget the hood) because it's too cold for anything else and it might rain, I feel like my clothes are shouting "tally-ho!", "yee-ha!", "respec'" and "run for cover!" all at the same time. I am wearing what I need in order to be practical, not what I want to wear.

That said, there are times when I manage to park the car

back home and walk to collect my daughter after a day in the office where I have worn clothes that I enjoy and that don't make me look like I've run through a fancy-dress shop. This fixes the 'look' issue. But walking half a mile in heels takes much longer than in flats and when combined with wearing your favourite Hobbs number and living in a village, you do feel slightly conspicuous as you trip-trap your way down a street on which there are no offices. It does also offer many opportunities to go over on your ankle which takes you back to when you were fourteen and practising walking in 'grown-up' shoes.

So, as I am about to embark on properly going back to work, and this may become a more regular occurrence, and I'm not about to start wear trainers with tights, I've decided there's only one thing for it. I'm getting a chauffeur. Bring on the gown!

Soundtrack: 'What a Girl Wants' - Christina Aguilera

4 LOVE, LOVE, LOVE

Romantic love, red hot love and everlasting love. It's all in this chapter.

LOVE IS CONTAGIOUS

After the Olympic torch relay tweet mentioned in my 'No Sex Please' post, a few people have asked me what prompted it, so here goes.

I was waiting with the children at a mini-roundabout by the Travelodge in Newbury (glamorous - n'est-ce pas?), for the spectacle to arrive. We'd chosen the spot because a group of people had set up camp there hours earlier so we reckoned it must be a good viewing place. Not for nothing do people risk catching their fingers in collapsible seating, fill flasks with hot tea and don cagoules. As we waited, a lovely couple explained that everyone was there for one torch bearer, Emma Cope, a 16-year-old local girl who had chosen to respond to her incurable kidney disease by fundraising for research. Her current total stands just shy of £38,000 and people were looking forward to publicly celebrating her incredible achievement.

The crowd got deeper and whilst I usually pride myself on my strength:size ratio, I couldn't lift both of my children at once without risking injury to one or all of us, and was struggling to give them a good view. My dilemma was picked up on by a lovely couple who offered to move out of the way so the children could stand at the front. This little display of generosity sparked further gestures as other members of Emma's party handed the children flags and braved the throngs of people reaching for giveaways to collect gymnastics ribbons and other goodies.

When Emma did arrive, her torch was not lit. She had been dropped off to await the 'mother flame', and stood for a second as if she had been teleported from another dimension - wide-eyed in a space-age tracksuit complete with mystical symbol (or golden cheese-grater, take your pick) in hand. A moment later her mum raced to her side and hugged her, which made everyone hug each other, which made us all a bit teary eyed.

From having Thames Valley Police as a warm-up act (I can't imagine I will again see a policeman on a motorbike conduct a cheering competition, then high-five spectators), to the kindness of strangers, to a mother's hug setting everyone off, it was a fantastic and memorable couple of hours where people were really happy together. It had flashing lights and whistles - all it would have needed was some techno, and people massaging each other's shoulders to have made it feel like a rave c.1991. Oh, and some people off their faces - but it was the middle of the day in Newbury, so it felt more like a rave held by a church group and the WI. Anyway, I digress - back to the point:

The feeling seemed to permeate the whole of the town. It even reached the man behind the voice that floated out of the parking payment machine. I had lost my ticket in the crowd and instead of charging me the £12 he should have for a lost ticket, he let me off. The good vibes of that day must have been contagious; I hope that it lasts way beyond the end of the Olympics.

Soundtrack: 'Love is Contagious' – Taja Sevelle

SUMMER NIGHTS

This week the sunshine has put in a proper appearance and brought happiness in many forms; children leaping into paddling pools or with hands held high like little chimps as mummy and daddy help them take their first steps into the sea, and everyone consuming more ice cream than seems sensible. The evening light becomes magical to run and cycle in, and convertible owners have 'got their tops off' to treat themselves to the sun on their shoulders, and pedestrians to the benefit of their musical tastes. *Note to the gentleman in the Volvo C70 driving through the village: 'Lady in Red' does* ***not*** *count as a summer song.*

The weather has also meant alfresco dining, cheeky early evening drinks at the pub and noise...lots of noise.

Some of the noise is welcome, like the sound of children playing, cockerels crowing and lawnmowers, but some of it is less so. The conversation between the builders at the bottom of our road is very funny to me, but I don't necessarily want the children to hear that by the time 'Dave' has "finished the f***ing chimney" someone "will have already moved in and lit a fire at the bottom of it!"

On particularly fine evenings we have quad bikes steaming past our house and up towards the Ridgeway. After the initial trip down memory lane to holidays spent zipping around the Greek islands on a scooter, it becomes very annoying and keeps us awake. Then it stops and just as you are about to fall asleep a mosquito sets up a one-man band next to your ear - how can something so miniscule be so loud?

This however was put into perspective by a friend who posted on Facebook that he was being included in his neighbour's bedroom antics by virtue of them flinging open the windows to let in some air whilst forgetting that it also let her yodelling all the way out of their window, down the road, and into other people's houses. She was evidently enjoying herself or was perhaps, we speculated, under the tuition of a vocal coach seeking to eke out her inner Mariah Carey. Much online hilarity ensued with suggestions that the lady having all the fun should be given some competition or a hearty round of applause when it ended or perhaps everyone on the thread should feel inspired to shut down their computer and find out if they could encourage their loved one to make the same amount of noise. It's good to know your neighbours are still getting their rocks off but you don't necessarily want the aural proof slipping through your window and into the lounge (or, as it sounded in this instance, slamming your front door open, charging down the hall, and rattling the glassware).

Funny as it was to read online, I realised two things.

- I was glad the only noise I had to contend with that evening was my neighbour's children shouting with delight as you do when you're nine and allowed to stay up late.

- I can live with the quad bikes.

Soundtrack: 'Summer Nights' - John Travolta & Olivia Newton John

ALL THE SMALL THINGS

Here are some things that have been the cause of bickering and exasperated cries in our house over the years:

Leaving a light on

Not loading the dishwasher 'correctly'

Not replacing the toilet roll

Leaving clothes on the floor

Choosing wallpaper

Why is it that these inconsequential things can be the cause of such frustration? How is it that a dropped plate can be the catalyst for actual tears? Why does stubbing your toe provoke a response more suited to a footballer feigning an injury?

Sometimes the little things can cause big outbursts and being an emotional type who wants life to be an endless festival of amusing distractions, I know I am guilty of overreacting and sometimes having unrealistic expectations.

Thankfully, however, I have great friends that are happy to discuss life without putting up a wall of pretence. During a particularly fruitful wine-assisted conversation we gave each other a good talking to on the fact that if you're in agreement on the massive stuff like marriage and raising the children then, in the grand scheme of things, the occasional expression of annoyance really is small fry. It would be unrealistic to expect to live with the same person for the rest of your life without ever having raised your voice or disagreed about whose turn it is to put the bins out.

So whilst one of us buying the 'wrong' type of crisps or forgetting to put Parent's Evening on the calendar may still cause a childish outburst or an "argh!" cry of frustration, I will take it in context and move on. I will try not to sweat the small stuff.

Soundtrack: All the Small Things – blink-182

I THINK WE'RE ALONE NOW

First Prince Harry is snapped playing billiards naked, then Kate and William get caught having some private time on holiday, and now The Queen has part of what she thought was a private conversation published. You think 'what goes on tour, stays on tour' and your mates take a picture of you with your tadger out and send it to everyone. You think that you're on a private balcony and someone takes a photo with a long lens and sells it to the papers. You think you're having a private conversation and it gets reported.

What a nightmare it must be. Imagine that you can't enjoy the sun on your skin or perhaps feel a little frisky in the sun with your loved one without someone desperate to take a photo and make money out of it. Imagine not feeling totally sure that your conversation is not going to be shared with the rest of the world. I was going to say, "imagine not being able to enjoy playing a game where the penalty for losing is nudity", but I don't feel I'm qualified to comment on how wonderful that appears to feel for vast swathes of men. The stories I have heard from friends who played club cricket and rugby about how waving your willy about, or tucking it between your legs, for the entertainment of others is so marvellously amusing still mystify me. Instead I would say imagine not being able to enjoy a night out without fear of it being broadcast to a waiting world.

We are all at risk of this to a much lesser degree: most of us probably have pictures published on Facebook that we'd rather the world didn't see, have said things that have gone on to be told to others that we would have preferred to keep private, or have been caught out in more - ahem - intimate moments (see '*Summer Nights*' for more on that).

The guidance to avoid all of this of course is to not do

anything that could possibly get us into trouble or be misconstrued. Therefore Kate and William should not be a young couple on holiday, Harry not be a bloke having a laugh with his mates and the Queen should not ask a question.

I'm not a subscriber to 'Majesty Magazine' or even a particularly fervent supporter of the Royal Family, but I do imagine what this must feel like for them as people. Watching what has gone on over the past few weeks has made me very grateful for the freedom to cock-up, trip-over, and have fun that I have. I intend to do more of it.

Soundtrack: 'I Think We're Alone Now' - Tiffany

LET'S TALK ABOUT SEX

So the Church of England has decided that gay men in civil partnerships can become bishops. Very good! But they must promise to be celibate - what?!

Now I make no claim to understand the politics and ancient traditions of the church but what I do know is that this decision seems to be creating a very strange condition of employment and one that I am wondering how on earth the church will enforce. My mind swims with images of senior clergy hiding in cupboards ready to leap out at the slightest hint of romance and spot-checks to make sure that the three-drawer chest is wedged securely between the single beds.

I agree with Rev Ian Stubbs comment[1] that it is odd to be told it's ok to be in a loving relationship but that you cannot express it in a sexual way. This is even stranger still if this judgement on your relationship comes from your employers who, in almost all other walks of life, would be deemed to be discriminating against you if they used your sexual preferences against you when deciding your capacity or suitability for a job.

Can you imagine working all your life to become an astronaut, or a brain surgeon, or a prima ballerina to be told that you can have the job, but only if you stop having sex? Actually, would you take any job where that was one of the requirements? Whether you get your rocks off on a daily basis or only fancy it on your birthday and Christmas, and whether you do it out of true love, for kicks, or to create new life, it is part of what makes us human so how can you be expected to switch it off?

I'll be interested to see how this goes. Perhaps all the

candidates *will* be celibate, and for those that aren't, I think there might be another ancient tradition involved that is still very much alive today: that of crossing your fingers when making a promise (plenty of space to do that in a cassock).

Soundtrack: 'Let's Talk About Sex' - Salt-N-Pepa

1 Source: http://www.bbc.co.uk/news/uk-20918806

THE LOOK OF LOVE

The wedding for which I purchased special underwear (as mentioned in 'Spanx for the Memories') was a triumph. As you would expect it was filled with joy, happiness, and a room full of people sincerely wishing the couple all the very best for their future together.

The attention to detail was incredible: retro sweets to inspire a sense of fun, a photo and video booth to capture everyone's congratulatory messages in real time (and to give the exhibitionists a safe place to bare their bottoms at midnight) and place settings made out of wooden hearts on pieces of string that the ladies tied to their wrists to add a romantic twist to their outfits. There was even a dedication on each table to loved ones now gone and heart-shaped confetti that had been painstakingly cut out of books of romantic poetry. Every tiny piece seemed to have a word like 'cherish' printed on it.

But the thing that really did it for me was when the groom was delivering a very emotional part of his speech, acknowledging the love he had not just for his wife and their son but also asking everyone to raise a toast to absent friends. At that point in time, with him and half the room in tears, his wife was calm and looking at him in a way that said "when you feel weak I will be strong." Theirs is truly a love match. It reminded me that outside of all of the things that we think we need and the money that we spend on baubles and parties to demonstrate our love (I love a diamond - don't get me wrong), there are times when a look like that says it better than anything else ever could.

Soundtrack: 'The Look of Love' – Dusty Springfield

LABELLED WITH LOVE

So the Olympics is almost upon us and the excitement levels are ratcheting up every day as the clock counts down and the media coverage increases. At our daughter's school the project for this term is, naturally, the Olympics and we've been having great fun completing and documenting mini sporting tasks and learning facts and figures about Team GB - I hadn't anticipated how much her homework would be a means for us to do things together so it is a welcome bonus! In class they are being taught about the Olympic and Paralympic values of respect, excellence, friendship, courage, determination, inspiration and equality which is giving them a fantastic opportunity to tackle some fairly big and important subjects.

What I hadn't anticipated was a discussion that included the assertion that "Cerrie on CBeebies would be in the Paralympics because she is disabled." I don't yet know in what context the word was introduced but it for me it is too early.

We have been CBeebies fans in our house for years and whilst the children have noticed that Cerrie has one hand, we have never called her disabled because the straightforward explanation that we are all made differently was enough. My brother has Down's Syndrome and to date we have not discussed his condition with the children because they quite simply do not see a difference that is worth remarking on at this point in time. The children just see their uncle and it had not occurred to me until recently how important it is for that to remain the case for as long as possible - unlike others, they view him without preconception or prejudice.

I understand that we need a common language to explain,

organise, and make sense of things. But now my daughter has a concept of difference that many people would term a 'label' and for what purpose? This is something that we did not introduce and may not have been necessary for a little while yet. So what to do? We've decided to deal with the questions as they come, but for as long as we can, we'll be keeping our house label-free.

Soundtrack: 'Labelled With Love' - Squeeze

DADDY COOL

With Father's Day just behind us now seems like a good time for a post on fatherhood.

I have heard that a man out with his children will be viewed by women as more attractive than a man out on his own. Now this really does depend on the setting; a father in a nightclub with his five-year-old twins, or a man hitchhiking with a baby might not support this theory...but if the father and child are in the right place, the theory could hold true.

When I met my husband we were in our twenties and spent our time and money on clubbing, drinking and eating out. We took our hangovers to work and started our weekends on a Thursday night. We went on long, expensive holidays, laid the foundations for years of in-jokes with our friends and generally did as we pleased for a good ten years.

You think at the time that it's the best it's going to get. What more could you want but to have no ties, cash in the bank and weekends dedicated to getting silly and falling over with your mates?

Fast forward to a wet Bournemouth beach on New Year's Day in 2005. We are married, I am nearly 30 and we decided that we would like to have children. 18 months later it becomes a reality and whilst there are a million other blog posts that could be written on the topic of parenthood, what a life affirming thing it is to see your husband hold his child for the first time.

Seeing your other half comfort and nurture a tearful toddler, wipe up the unspeakable (and sometimes unstoppable) mess that comes from every orifice of a newborn, pull ridiculous faces to get that first gurgling giggle, mend bikes, play catch, sit through Mr Tumble for the tenth time, tie little laces, learn lullabies and sit on a child's chair at parent's evening with a straight face is, for me at least, one of the most fantastic parts of parenting. For all the DIY, heavy-lifting, log-splitting and fire making skills a man may have, there is something perhaps even more masculine in being a great father. Which brings us back to the start - seeing a man who is great with his children is a better advert for masculinity than a man with his shirt off showing you how 'ripped' he is. Fact.

Soundtrack: 'Daddy Cool' – Boney M

NOT FORGOTTEN

Last year I went to the funeral of a friend who had died, suddenly and unexpectedly, leaving behind three beautiful young children, a heartbroken husband and countless friends who struggled to believe that she was no longer there. At the service her husband and children showed incredible strength as they told us about her life, how rich she had made their lives and how positively she touched the people around her. It was a humbling experience.

As part of the service, each of us had been given a card to write down our memories of her for the family to keep as a tribute. It caused us all to reflect on our shared histories, the great times that we'd had, and in writing them down, we turned them into a permanent record. When speaking to her husband a few months later, he said that these cards, and the letters that he had received from friends that spoke of picnics, pub trips, chaotic days out with the children and dancing on chairs to 'Sunshine Mountain', had brought him great comfort and some happiness because it proved what he always knew. His wife was beautiful, kind hearted, fun-loving, thoughtful and someone that would never be forgotten. These letters and cards will help the children know more about their mum, give them an insight into the girl and woman that she was, and hopefully along the way provide them with stories that they find hilarious, awe-inspiring and comforting.

I hadn't appreciated the impact of this type of remembrance until very recently. After putting a picture of my dad in a previous blog post, a friend left a comment on my Facebook page that read "Bless your dad Toni...so remember him xx". It's just seven words, but they made my day. Twenty-two years on, that acknowledgement of his life is still a meaningful and powerful thing. So if you know somebody that has lost someone they love - let them know that you remember too.

5 WORKING NINE TO FIVE

Considering how much time I've spent at work throughout my life so far, this chapter is remarkably short. But it does cover the most important topics: Getting paid, dealing with Neanderthals and what to do if confronted with a sauna full of naked people.

PAID IN FULL

I'm willing to wager that people who design pay and incentive plans for large businesses do not have children, or if they do, they can't get them to make their beds.

Before becoming a freelancer my 'package' was made up of salary, and a bonus plan so complex that it required knowledge of database technology to find out on what deals you had been paid. Add to that an annual review with a scoring system of 1-5, and the requirement to complete CBIs, KPIs and meet an RBI, and you can understand why many people thought it was SH**. I'll let you complete the rest.

Compare this to encouraging a child to get themselves ready in the morning. During a conversation with some friends (as mentioned in the *'Because You're Worth It'* post), one remarked how her children aged four and seven not only made their beds but also tidied their rooms, made breakfast and got themselves dressed without complaining. They may be dressed in a tutu, a t-shirt, and a pair of their dad's socks, but they did it by themselves. The friend got them to do this through the well-worn tactic of a reward chart and pocket money. The rest of us mused on the fact that we had become incredibly slack and resolved to make some changes in our own homes.

Summer holiday out of the way, we decided to go for it and already the children are doing a list of things that historically would have taken much nagging to achieve. Our daughter loves being in charge of making breakfast and our son is constantly asking what else he can do to get more stars. They're even putting their clothes in the washing basket which is something that not all of the adults in the house achieve.

Going through this reward process has made me realise that there are times as adults in business when we allow ourselves to be treated like lab rats: made to carry out increasingly complicated (and often, meaningless) tasks in order to receive rewards whilst layers of management watch over spreadsheets that we are made to populate to record our progress against nebulous KPIs). Leaving that environment meant that I avoided the headache that is an annual review conducted in algebra. I also have a true sense of the value and worth of the work that I do for my clients. I do a good job, and they pay me. Simple eh?

It feels like a proper, grown-up way to conduct business and it certainly motivates me to work harder than any incentive plan ever did. I'm not saying that businesses need to set up sticker charts in their offices, but I do think that a lot of companies could learn from the simplicity of providing an easy-to-understand programme that rewards a few critical things done exceptionally well, rather than an access database of metrics that takes a year to figure out. It might make their staff feel like they're being treated a bit more like adults when it comes to getting paid.

Soundtrack: 'Paid in Full' - Eric B & Rakim

IT'S DIFFERENT FOR GIRLS

I am watching a webcast designed to discuss and promote the role of women in IT featuring contributions from female business owners and senior execs. They are going to share their success stories and advise us on how to encourage more girls to consider a career in the sector. So far, so inspiring. Until four minutes in one of the panel says "being a woman in IT is hard because we have to manage so many things, like doing the shopping" . *LIKE DOING THE SHOPPING?!* One small sentence for a woman, one giant negative stereotype for womankind.

The rest of the webcast was useful but I bet there were people that switched off at that point. Possibly it was an indicator of her domestic set-up and probably she didn't intend it to sound the way it did but it made my heart sink. Of all the challenges that I have seen and experienced as a woman working in the IT industry, 'doing the shopping' doesn't even make the list.

The actual challenges I've experienced sit in two camps:

Encounters with cavemen:

> The newly appointed sales director who said on my first meeting with him to discuss my career: "If I was a customer and you came into my office, I'd think you were a secretary."
>
> The finance manager who, when I told him I didn't want to buy a car on finance, thought he could change my mind by saying: "But *even housewives* can get finance."
>
> The regional director who said to my manager

"How can you concentrate with *that* in the office?" and winked.

Encounters with uninformed people:

Such as the pupils I met at a careers day who were asked to guess what job I did. They guessed 'a secretary, or a nurse, or veterinary assistant, or a shop assistant, or a primary school teacher'. I wouldn't mind but for the fact that they had a description of what my job involved. Their guesses were based on what jobs they thought women generally do.

The cavemen referred to in the first camp seem to subscribe strongly to the 'Al Murray, The Pub Landlord' view of suitable careers for women and are unlikely to be swayed. I decided not to work for the first person, I didn't buy from the second person, and the third: well I was twenty at the time and not really sure what to do about it so I ignored him. Hopefully they will wake up when their daughters are earning more than them.

Where the cavemen are often better ignored, I think we can do something about the uninformed people. If we can encourage more girls to consider IT and let them see that coding is cool, or if coding's not their thing that there are hundreds of other interesting jobs in sales, marketing, finance, training and support then we might start to see the tide change. Yes, some of the job descriptions are a bit nebulous (made up even), and a lot of the jobs are not as socially useful or important as other professions and trades, but there are children who may miss out on life-transforming opportunities because they have a narrow view of the world of work.

So how do we make sure that the next generation of girls joining the workplace know there is a place for them in IT?

If you are a woman in IT and you love what you do, please lend your voice to encourage more girls to join in, whether supporting a careers event at your old school, or becoming involved in a group like DigiGirlz (google it for your local group), joining one of the 'Women in IT' social networks (www.womenintechnology.co.uk) or checking out the work of the pioneering Little Miss Geek (www.littlemissgeek.org). Talk, tweet, network and blog about it, tell people you're 'IT and Proud!'. Let's start inspiring and sod the shopping!

Soundtrack: 'It's Different for Girls' - Joe Jackson

LOST IN TRANSLATION

Part of my day job is delivering training courses. It's something that I started doing after becoming a freelancer and is one of my favourite things to do as it plays to my love of standing up in front of a crowd and helping other people. It also offers the opportunity for new and interesting experiences like the time I delivered a course in Prague.

I had a class of 25 people from seven different countries to train, all of whom spoke English as their second language. We calculated that between them they spoke 13 different languages - and I spoke just the one. It was nerve-racking at first but with some patience, willingness, and good humour, we spent the first day together discussing the finer points of financial statements and I went back to the hotel feeling it had been a good job, well done.

With the evening to myself and the hotel boasting a gym and pool I thought I'd head downstairs for a swim. The receptionist informed me that there was an aqua aerobics class taking place but that I didn't have to participate if I didn't want to. I only wanted to do a few lengths but the 'pool' as it turned out was only ten metres long and full of women waiting for their workout to begin. As I couldn't very well hop on an exercise bike in my swimming costume without causing hilarity or offence, and as the aqua aerobics instructor was motioning for me to take an empty spot between two depressingly attractive Czech ladies I had no choice but to join in.

Tables now turned from the day's training, I had to rely on reading the instructor's movements to tell me precisely how I was supposed to combine the floats, weights, and arm and leg movements to exercise without drowning myself. He stood poolside, shouting instructions in Czech and showing us what we were supposed to be doing. The challenge (apart from the language barrier) was that he was on 'dry land' and we were in the pool so when we were supposed to be lifting two legs, he could only lift one. Once I caught on to this fact things started to go a little better and the rest of the lesson passed without incident or embarrassment.

Impromptu aerobics over, I thought I'd treat myself to a sauna but what I had failed to remember is that we in the UK are a somewhat uptight nation and of course, the way you sauna throughout the rest of Europe is in the nude. All I can say is thank heavens for glass doors as it afforded me the opportunity to see the occupants and make a quick swerve away from the door with a look of mild alarm on my face rather than entering a sauna full of butt-naked people. The swerve did not go unnoticed however, and through that one movement and without a word spoken I was saying "I AM BRITISH AND I DO NOT SAUNA IN MY BIRTHDAY SUIT!"

Think this was the last of my communication challenges that day? Think again...

After having some dinner and returning to my room I thought I'd check my presentation slides for the following day. Now, one of the most useful items you can have as a presenter or trainer is a 'clicker'. It gives you the freedom to move about the room and control the presentation rather than having to stay at your laptop. It is a key piece of equipment for me and as I was wandering up and down my hotel room practising, the clicker stopped working. Not good. I figured out that it had run out of juice and so called reception to explain that I specifically needed two AAA batteries. They said they would check and duly called me back to say 'yes, they did have some and would I like to come down and collect them?' I dashed down, the receptionist handed them over and said I was very lucky as they were the last two and then gave me a bit of a funny look that involved a half smile and a raised eyebrow. I smiled broadly, thanked her profusely and then skipped off back to my room. And then I realised what that funny look was for. It was 10.00pm and I had dashed down to reception to collect some AAA batteries and been really happy about getting them. I didn't tell her I had a broken clicker, but that look on her face told me exactly what she thought the batteries were for.....

6 CHILDREN

Being the parent of two small children, and having vivid memories of my own childhood, means a lot of my writing time is dedicated to figuring out how I can do a better job of being a parent and the best way in which to avoid my children reliving my teenage years, as well as marvelling at just what you are able to put up with at the dinner table. Would you like some regurgitated carrot with your Sunday lunch or would you prefer the 'pausing to wipe a smelly bottom' option?

WE DON'T NEED NO EDUCATION?

Our daughter is about to finish her second year of primary school and we are in awe of what the teachers have helped her to achieve. There are so many moments that we want to wrap up and hold on to: stories written with the most hilarious spellings (and mostly involving wolves having their stomachs cut open to allow villagers to escape), drawings of us all holding hands and early attempts at times tables. She is in her element and we are loving watching her learn. This is rubbing off on our son. He loves the fact he has 'lessons' at pre-school and can't wait to join his sister so that he can have his own book bag and uniform.

In my last years at senior school it would be fair to say that I didn't care too much for education. I left with a couple of As but also a couple of Fs and a few other letters in between. I started work on my 16th birthday in a fruit and veg shop that paid £68 a week cash in hand. I thought I was loaded and very much enjoyed attempting to pay for half a lager and lime with a £50 note at the local pub. The landlord did not share my hilarity but he liked the money my friends and I brought in, so we were tolerated. It didn't take long, however, for me to realise that spending my days in a green and white tabard serving bananas to bodybuilders and potatoes to pensioners was not going to get me very far. This was further underlined by friends popping in during my shift and bellowing "Have you got any caulies?!" much to the dismay of my manager. There's nothing like shrieking 16-year-olds to scare away the high-spending old ladies.

So I enrolled at college where I was completely won over by my new experience of education. Not only could I choose subjects based on what I thought I'd like to study but I was also allowed to call the teachers by their first names -

winner! The most important thing for me though was that it gave me a chance to enjoy learning again. Sitting in a class with a group of people who have chosen to attend is a very different sensation to being in a class because it is a legal requirement for you to be there. There was a slight hiccup though, in that having completed my 'A' Levels (and re-sat my Maths GCSE), I asked the careers advisor what I could do next. Her response was "you can apply for university." This was not an option as I had no money and didn't fancy racking up debts, but fortunately she enrolled me on a secretarial course where I learned how to turn up on time and touch-type. Before the end of the first year I had my first 'proper' job.

Because of the teachers Basingstoke College of Technology, I rediscovered the pleasure of learning, and gained practical skills that set me on a path to opportunities and experiences I couldn't have imagined as a sullen sixteen-year-old. I thank them for setting me right.

Our children are at the very beginning of their journey. I know that there will be ups and downs in their time at school, and whether they choose to become academics or apprentices, roofers or rock-stars, I will work my hardest to keep and encourage the love of learning that they have today for the rest of their lives.

Soundtrack: 'The Wall' – Pink Floyd

THE KIDS ARE ALRIGHT

Sullen, unruly, unpredictable, disrespectful, angry, smelly, noisy, reckless. Full of rage, passion, wanting everything for nothing but most of all wanting to be LEFT ALONE! Ah the life of a teenager. Tricky years for everyone involved and I did apologise to my mum for mine. She said "It's ok, I knew you'd get it out of your system eventually." One very forgiving mother.

Confidence boosted, I apologised to a teacher at our official ten-year school reunion as it had occurred to me that I might not have been a joy to teach. Her reply was "It's a bit late for that." In hindsight, I think she was biting her tongue and just about resisting the urge to put me in a headlock and knuckle-rub my scalp for being such a pain in the arse. Sorry (again) Mrs C and the rest of the teaching staff for my conduct during those final two years.

But hang on a minute: this is in defence of teenagers and so what I really want to say is this:

For all of the above, and for the graffiti, shouting, swearing, pocketing of Mars Bars, staying out all night, lying about where you are / have been / are going, failing to call home, hanging about on the street with your mates and the poor choice of boyfriends/girlfriends/clothes – "Call *that* a skirt?!" For all the underage drinking, smoking and for all the stuff you would rather not know about, I do know this:

As a teenager, despite stating loudly (and frequently) "I'm fine", I remember being pretty ill-equipped to deal with some of the 'grown-up shit' that tends to happen in life such as serious illness, death, disability, and having to decide precisely what I was going to do once free of school, so my outlet was sometimes at odds with what most people would deem as 'acceptable' behaviour.

But eventually, like most of my friends, I worked it out, grew up, moved on, and hoped that nobody took photos of the really embarrassing stuff. I am forever grateful that my generation enjoyed its youth before the advent of phones with cameras, and the only people that took pictures were the ones interested in photography.

It is easy to criticise the behaviour of teenagers, to look down on them and to conveniently gloss over our own misspent youth. For those who did just that to the group of teenagers I was part of, I hope they will be pleased to know we have grown up to become artists, teachers, photographers, housing officers, fundraisers, chefs, business owners, volunteers, and parents that would, and do, set their own needs aside for those of their children. It was just a phase and we did alright in the end.

I have quite a few years to go until I have the pleasure (?) of being a parent to teenage children, but I hope that when the time comes, I will be mindful of my own journey in supporting them to make theirs. That, and that they'll be model teens who do the Duke of Edinburgh Award Scheme, play music that I like, and never get into trouble. If not, I'd better brace myself...

Soundtrack: 'The Kids are Alright' - The Who

THE THINGS WE DO FOR LOVE

We are at lunch one Sunday. There's me, my husband, the two kiddlies (aged four and two at the time) and our friends with their little boy who is six months old. We are chatting, reminiscing, laughing at how our life stages can be mapped by the changes to the ways in which we socialise together.

Singletons: Pub straight after work then out clubbing until someone realises that it is the next day, we're still in yesterday's clothes, and we really ought to go home.

Established / Married Couples: Pub, followed by a restaurant, then back to someone's for more drinks until someone remembers that sleeping on the floor is really bloody uncomfortable and that we have got a comfy bed at home.

Babies: Sunday lunch. Sod the pub, we're too tired and can't find a babysitter.

We elected to eat at our friends' house this time as while taking a baby to a pub can work, taking mobile, extremely noisy children is a risky and expensive business. Also, our friends had access to CBeebies, which guarantees you at least 30 minutes of peace to try to vaguely catch up on each other's lives.

The dinner is delish and the children are behaving nicely. It feels civilised, relaxed, really enjoyable. And then the baby pukes all over his highchair, down himself, and a little bit onto his dad's sleeve. Forks are lowered, conversation stops. Nobody puts food in their mouth for we are in the presence of hot baby sick.

Dad picks his son up, wipes him clean, cleans the highchair, wipes his sleeve and we all carry on eating. Parenting makes you properly hardcore like that. No expulsion, explosion, stink or stench stops a meal for longer than it takes to clean up said mess.

We eat some more, laugh some more and agree that we have to do some pretty grim things as part of loving and caring for our children. And then, just as we've started on the pudding, my son's voice comes loud and clear from the downstairs loo: "Muuuh-meeee I've fi-niiiiiiiished." I sigh, put down my spoon and head to my smelly destiny.
Now *that's* love.

Soundtrack: 'The Things we do for Love' - 10cc

WITH THE ILL BEHAVIOUR

So we returned from our half-term break refreshed, revitalised and having almost achieved a tech-free holiday (if you don't count the TV) but wondering about something. Why is it that our darling angels pick being on holiday with other people as the best time to try out their worst behaviour? In the past few shared holidays that we've had there have been inordinate amounts of tantrums, shouting and point blank refusals to do as they're told. Nothing more serious than that but a very tiring state of affairs and just a little bit embarrassing.

There are plenty of explanations: they are excited, they are with their friends, they are free from the stricture of routines imposed by school and pre-school and the set way that we do things at home. It always surprises us when we get back how much calmer they seem but if you factor in the point that mum and dad are not nearly as interesting as their friends and their normal routine does not involve going to the beach every day and getting to stay up late then it does make sense. Equipped with such knowledge we now know to brace ourselves and try to relax a bit so they don't feel that for the entire holiday their surnames have been changed to "No" or "Stop it!"

Then a few days ago a friend was telling me that during the wee small hours of a particularly lively dinner party she was holding, her 19-year-old daughter got out of bed and stood at the top of the stairs to tell her off for making too much noise. Tables turned, here was the parent being the naughty one, and classically she responded with a "No, I will not!" It was payback time.

It made me think about what happens when I get together with my friends. Some of this is documented (see 'Doing it for the Kids' or 'The Kids are Alright') but I will also take this opportunity, in the spirit of reminding myself that it isn't just the children who muck around, to confess to participating in the following:

- A re-enaction of a 'Spaghetti Western' using tinned spaghetti as our weapon of choice (out of the tin of course, we weren't animals!).

- Making phone calls on behalf of the fictitious 'Friendly Society' which involved calling people to wish them a Happy New Year. Whilst our calls were unexpected, we did get a lot of bewildered people saying "Thank You"!

- Having a fruit and veg fight in a classroom.

- Calling out to strangers from a moving car asking them in an anguished voice "When are you coming home?"

- Stuffing a car - including the glove compartment - full of leaves.

- Whining at a DJ for switching the music off because we just want to dance, man!

I have also witnessed people eating the entire contents of sugar bowls, thirty olives in one go, massively over-spiced curries (sometimes by choice, other times spiked) and pots of mustard for fun. It's one thing to muck about but I draw the line at inflicting pain on my intestines - I'll leave that to the cast iron stomachs of my male friends.

All of this is silly, childish behaviour fuelled by being with friends and often by one too many shandies. Replace the shandies with industrial amounts of ice cream and orange juice and you have the perfect small person's storm.

So there it is: it's not just the children. The desire to muck about is in all of us, it's just that for the most part our children are spared the embarrassment of our misbehaviour. Next holiday I'll cut them a bit more slack.

Soundtrack: 'Renegade Master' – Wildchild

I READ THE NEWS TODAY, OH BOY

In the week that Lord Leveson released his report on press regulation and the media is awash with comment and opinion on a free press; our daughter has become a 'free reader'.

To be a 'free reader' is a much coveted title at school; it means that you no longer have to follow a colour-coded reading book programme but can instead select any book that you like from the school library. We are justly proud of our daughter, and delighted with her teachers.

Her confidence increased, she has taken to reading anything that she can see, whether it's intended for her or not. As a result, she has given us cause to reconsider where we leave our reading material more than once this week.

It began with her asking us who the man on the front of Private Eye was, then reading aloud the contents of his speech bubble. She was disappointed to discover that the 'cover star' Lord Leveson is not related to Father Christmas because his outfit "looks almost the same." It's a fair point but as interested as she was, we're not entirely sure she's ready for political critique and satire and so we've put it out of her reach.

This was followed by our son pointing out that there was a picture in the paper of 'Mary and Joseph'. It was, in fact, an image of three Afghanistani women. Taken on its own, it is a funny and understandable mistake for a child to make but for the fact that the accompanying story was about the murder of a young girl for refusing an arranged marriage. Our daughter wanted to read the story. Another paper gets put out of the way.

My husband and I have agreed to make sure that we put anything that's not for little eyes out of sight and we think that we're doing ok. And then I go to a shop in a nearby village where there is apparently great demand for 'adult' magazines. I don't know what the legislation is on front covers, but apparently as long as there are stars over a woman's nipples then it is fine for it to be in plain view, even if she is attempting to lick the star off or is pointing at another part of her constellation-covered anatomy.

As a child, *The Sun* was the favoured daily paper of my parents so rarely a day passed where I didn't see which 'lovely' had her baps out for the delectation of the British public. There was also a stash of 'dirty magazines' always left in the local woods (with the Internet not yet invented people took to the wilds with nothing but a magazine, a hanky and a furtive look) so I did not grow up unaware of quite how fascinating the female form is to so many, but I don't want it for *my* children. You could argue that the magazines are out of their line of sight but that is to assume that they never look up or around them and that is also to assume that they cannot read. For whilst the woman's breasts came with the requisite stars, her bottom half was concealed by the legend: "Footy Fanny!" There is a part of me that wants to guffaw at its absolute shabbiness but as a mother I am appalled that a shop in the middle of a housing estate, and next to a nursery, is putting magazines like this just one display away from CBeebies magazine. Thankfully our daughter didn't get the opportunity to look in that direction as she was too busy being led away with me muttering something like "they've run out of sweets…"

I remember hearing a woman who had not learned to read until adulthood say during an interview that it had been like someone turning up the volume on the world. Whilst up until that point she had understood spoken conversation perfectly well, the wording on signs, in papers, on the sides of vans, cars and buses, and the back of tins and packets had always been silent to her. After learning to read she felt they were shouting out to grab her attention, crowding her brain with messages and urging her to read more. This is how it is now for our little 'free reader', and it's our responsibility to make sure as far as possible, it's only the good stuff that gets heard.

Soundtrack: 'A Day in the Life' - Neil Young, Live at Glastonbury 2009.

HOW SOON IS NOW?

I believe that the school Christmas holidays are designed by quantum physicists and contain a special ability to bend space-time in order to confuse the hell out of us. The children are bewildered as to what day it is and learning to cope with boredom despite being surrounded by Christmas presents, and parents are trapped in a fug of overindulgence from eating plate upon plate of rich, lovely, food and deciding it's a great idea to finish the night off with a double Baileys, and then a gin and tonic, and perhaps the last tree chocolate. And some Twiglets. And some port. And if the port's open then we might as well get the cheese out...feel your waistline expand overnight!

Our son returned to pre-school today and my husband has been working over the festive period but full equilibrium is not restored until I go back to work and our daughter goes back to school next week. I am trying my hardest to re-engage but it feels like an effort to even look at the laptop as the screen of choice for the past two weeks has been TV-sized for the never-ending feast of movies.

Getting up in the morning has drifted from the regimented to the frankly, slack. After the huge build up and early waking caused by the promise of presents and then the days spent eating more sugar than you will admit to their dentist and running around like a lunatic clutching toys as the tree lights flash in techno timing, the children are completely exhausted. First day back at school and work is going to require some serious prep and negotiation to make sure we get there on time and in the right clothing. It will be a very bad day indeed if she wears my leopard print kitten heels and I wear her princess dress.

Today, after venturing out to the shops to try to find something that is neither 40% saturated fat or 40% proof for our cupboards, our daughter said to me, "It feels like Sunday, doesn't it?" Quite right she was too, and it took us a few seconds to agree on what day it actually was but the question that hurt our brains the most was one posed by our son when he asked us: "Is today tomorrow?" This prompted a five minute conversation about how yes, if today were yesterday (which it wasn't) then today would indeed be tomorrow, but today is now today, which makes tomorrow tomorrow, and not today tomorrow because today was tomorrow but only when viewed from yesterday. At the end of this explanation (which to my mind was worthy of a pat on the back from Brian Cox although in fairness I think he's more of a hair-ruffler than a back-patter), he added neatly that if that were the case, then could he please have a chocolate from the tree. Because I'd told him yesterday that he could have one tomorrow.

So thank you, oh school timetable warlords, you have brought physics to the forefront of our conversations and inspired our son with science but if you wouldn't mind sending me a new copy of *A Brief History of Time* before the Easter holiday kicks in, I'd be very grateful.

Soundtrack: 'How Soon is Now' - The Smiths

HEY MAMA

Before the birth of our first child, I went with my husband to NCT lessons. Eight couples booked in for eight evening sessions with one earth-mother to guide us through what was to come using lots of props and an endless supply of her home-baked cookies.

Many of the things that she asked us to discuss and consider were very useful, and lots of the things that she said worked for me personally as a means to go into the business of childbirth feeling empowered and ready. But the rest of it was a blur of plastic babies that we had to pretend to breastfeed and change, little dollies wearing nappies containing various foodstuffs to show us what the first few weeks of poo should look like (I have never looked at mustard in the same way since). She also particularly enjoyed putting the husbands into awkward positions during role-play birth sequences such as when she had one of them up on a bed covered with stickers to represent the various tubes, monitors, and medieval implements that may be used in the escalation of childbirth interventions from forceps via ventouse to emergency C-section. Then there was the time when she made us link arms as a group to mimic the behaviour of the uterus and cervix during labour whilst she floated around in the middle waiting to 'be born'... sometimes I have to remind myself that actually did happen. It did. My husband has never quite recovered. I challenge you to come up with a more terrible team building experience.

What we didn't cover, and couldn't, was the experience of motherhood itself which I think was a great thing as we were already burdened with too many expectations that most of us would fail to live up to and couldn't be fixed by buying a changing bag emblazoned with Yummy Mummy -

whose bloody ridiculous and extremely patronising idea was that? I am glad to have given parenting magazines a wide berth and for taking the advice of a former manager which was to "buy the Gina Ford book and then burn it." I looked at one of the examples contained within the book of how to plan your day: there is no time to be a person in it except when you're asleep and dreaming of burning that book.

So we make it up as we go along, try to learn from our own mother's successes and mistakes and cross our fingers that we're doing a good job. With children that are still very young, I am only just on the journey but here's what I've found so far:

– Children rearrange your life, your priorities and your body.

– No outfit is made better by the addition of poo, sick or bogies.

– There is nothing quite like having a belly laugh with a five-year-old at the dinner table.

– I am glad I partied hard, travelled far, and established my career first.

– Old ladies really do stop you in the street to coo over the contents of your pram.

– Seeing your husband being a great dad is an incredibly attractive thing.

– Babies really do say "nom, nom, nom" when being fed.

- Sleep is the holy grail.

- I wish I could bottle up the greeting the children get from their grandma.

- The children might not understand the concept of 'today' and 'tomorrow' but they completely 'get' love. I heard a fantastic conversation on the playground where some of the children were discussing how marriage can be between men, women, or a man and a woman, as long as they love each other. It made my heart glad.

- The only prejudices they hold are ones that we put there.

- Watching the 'Baked Potato Song'[1] together as a means to revisit your teenage love of Vic and Bob whilst entertaining the children will turn it into a 'family song'.

There's loads more, I'm sure, but I think that'll do for starters. Oh, except for one thing, how beautiful they look when they're asleep. I think I'm going to go and gaze at them for a while - a real Mother's Day treat*.

Soundtrack: 'Hey Mama' – The Black Eyed Peas

**This post was composed on Mother's Day 2012.*

1 George Dawes on Shooting Stars sings the 'Baked Potato Song' here: http://www.youtube.com/watch?v=bPsY_nbTtxg

DOING IT FOR THE KIDS

I used to think that getting married was just about the couple involved. You meet each other, fall in love, there's a proposal (or tequila and falling down some stairs whilst attempting a fireman's carry in our case) and the rest of your lives together awaits you.

This has been challenged in recent years as more of my friends and relatives have married after having their children. Some met in their thirties and prioritised babies over tying the knot. For some, an important reason for marrying was to ensure they had the same surname as their children and, more poignantly, some married due to a diagnosis of cancer or to celebrate the great relief of an 'all clear this time' post-cancer check.

In almost every case, and in those where friends and relatives have had their marriages blessed, the children have been part of the ceremony. They have been ushers, bridesmaids, ring-bearers and generally the stars of the show. My nephew got to sign the register at the wedding of my sister-in-law and her husband. He was just five at the time and wrote his own place in his family's history - how cool is that?

My children often ask about our wedding day and we get the photos out and chat a bit about what happened. There are some things that we leave out, the half-naked man at the end (thank God it was the top half), the people in the unlocked bar helping themselves, the silver platter that went missing then re-surfaced a few years later at a friend's buffet, the 'naughty table' who had drinking games as their starter, and the person who asked if they could "crash in our room" because they had forgotten to book one and had run out of money. The answer to the last one was a resounding "no" accompanied by the throwing of money at the situation - what were they thinking? Let's just say it was a reception at which people got stuck in to the refreshments.

Around the time of our twelfth wedding anniversary, the conversation came up again and my daughter asked if I still had my wedding dress. When I said "yes", she pleaded with me until I agreed to get it down from the loft and then (after opening the two massive boxes and unravelling the reams of acid-free paper it was stored in) instructed me to put it on. Not that I minded - I had given up on the idea that either me or the girls would arrange a wedding dress party like the one Monica had in Friends, so it was good fun to wear it once again. And what a laugh we had. My daughter put on a party dress, my son put on his favourite Spiderman pants (well, what else would a modern page boy wear?), they picked up the train and we pranced around the house, up and down stairs and through the kitchen while they chanted "wedding, wedding, wedding!" My husband was bemused, although not entirely surprised. Being stuck in with the children on a rainy day often results in one of us being dressed up, painted on or 'turned into something' for their amusement.

Once the children felt suitably entertained, and they had coerced us into showing them our first dance (it was a classic - shuffling round in a circle with one or two twirls to make it look like we were putting in a bit of effort), the dress went back in its boxes and up into the loft. The shoes were put away and the discussion turned to more important questions like "do babies wear clothes when they're in their mummy's tummy?"

Our hour of make-believe was not quite a wedding, or a marriage blessing, but it was a lovely family moment and, if my husband would like to buy me another dress and some more diamonds maybe we'll do it for real? Actually I know the answer to that one, better pencil in a trip into the loft for 2024.

Soundtrack: 'Kids' - Robbie Williams and Kylie Minogue

SWEET CHILD O' MINE

During the course of a pre-Christmas clear-out I came across a box containing the tiny wristbands the children were issued with when they were born: little strips of plastic containing a lot of important information. Along with the relief that I will always have a record of precisely what time they were born (I confess I don't remember - a bit busy experiencing the 'special' sensation that comes with childbirth to check my watch - first time - and thinking "oh no! I remember this part and it's really horrible!" - second time -), was that they read 'baby of Toni Kent'.

So fast were the tags put on that their names were not recorded - and after all those months poring over name books and negotiating! They just 'belong' to their mother and exist as nothing else officially until you visit the registrar and hope that they don't make a mistake and register your little boy as 'Sue' or your little girl as 'Frank'.

Then come the family tours and the visits to work which boost the spirits and where nobody complains if the baby farts loudly or vomits on their black top but instead they congratulate you on managing to hold it together for long enough to get out of the house (even if you did have a little cry in the car, and another one in the loos, and you might have one on the way home) and how you've 'sprung back into shape' when in fact you have rolled your stomach up and stuffed it into a pair of control knickers. They might also remark on how much your offspring looks like you. Or not in my case, but that's ok, at least they won't ever be greeted with "ooh don't you look like your mum!" I've yet to meet an adult that feels 100% happy with that 'compliment'.

As the children grow they are testing boundaries and asserting themselves in ways that we hadn't predicted would happen so soon. Conversations at the dinner table switch from what happens after you've swallowed your food to what happens after you die, to precisely how old Yoda is. It is like being in constant preparation for a general knowledge quiz… and they don't always agree with, or accept, our answers.

Refusals of some kind happen on a daily basis: having their hair brushed, wearing something that looks vaguely smart (even weather-appropriate would do - our son wears shorts almost without exception), doing homework,
and sometimes we are not even permitted to hold our daughter's hand on the walk to school. At each turn we try to hide our frustration or sadness in the hope that they might do what we want or would like. Behaviour can be encouraged or resolved with a trip to the reward chart or the threat of pocket money deductions but on things like their opinion on what they wear or whether they feel like holding our hand we know we have to let them make their own decisions - we are kidding ourselves if we think we're in charge! Each day sees their personalities building and each year brings more independence of action and thought. They are growing up, and away from us.

We carry them round and cuddle them tight, calling them "mine" and "ours", take endless photos and videos and post status updates on their achievements, but they might grow up to be embarrassed by this, by us, and our delight in the minutiae of their youth. Remember the shame of your mum getting the baby photos out in front of your boyfriend or girlfriend? The school photos that were all over the living room wall charting the never-ending horror of the home-cut fringe? I like to look at them now but it's safe to say that my teenage self would have been quite happy for none to have existed as I strained at the leash to establish myself as appearing completely unrelated to my family.

Much as we love our children and give them everything we think they need, it's likely that at some point they're going to think we're cramping their style or being frankly rubbish parents. So I will try to see these little disagreements and differences of opinions as reasons to celebrate their individuality, be happy that they are building their own personality and hope that we are laying the right foundations for confident, independent, healthy, happy people (whilst secretly holding on to the hope that they will let us hug them tight and call them silly names well into their twenties!).

Soundtrack: 'Sweet Child O' Mine' - Guns N Roses

I CAN'T GET NO SLEEP

One of my friends had a beautiful baby girl a few weeks ago and posted the following on her Facebook page:

"I miss sleep! An uninterrupted full night's sleep with a lie-in is all I want for Xmas."

It made me remember how you don't appreciate just how brilliant sleep is until you are deprived of it over an extended period of time. For us, it was brought home very suddenly and forcefully when our daughter was born and of all the things that we thought we were prepared for, going without sleep wasn't one of them. The change from being able to make up for getting in at 3am by staying in bed until 2pm to being woken every two hours to then stay up feeding for an hour is pretty challenging and more than a little mood-altering. I am not ashamed to admit there were more than a couple of dark moments mixed in with the joy of our new arrival.

I was counselled by friends and relatives to sleep when the baby sleeps and, of course, completely ignored it because I was going to 'carry on as normal'. I scheduled myself silly but when it got to the point that I got lost on the way back from a hospital appointment (in the village where our daughter was born of all places) and had to call my husband to direct me home I knew that I had to listen to what these smart ladies (and my body) were saying.

Sometimes we need a reminder that there are times our body needs to rest for very good reason. There are times when we should switch off the phone, the PC, the outside world. My reminder was in the form of going round in circles in Wallingford for twenty minutes feeling like I had lost the plot. For other friends it was crying in the supermarket, being reminded by a bus driver that they needed to take their baby with them when they got off the bus and for some ticking 'those' boxes on the questionnaire you fill out at your six week check-up with the midwife.

But this is Reasons to be Cheerful and so I will end with another, happier, reminder. It was the joy of waking up after a delicious two hour nap that was gifted to me by my friend Nimisha when my daughter was about two months old. She arrived with a box full of home-made Indian sweets rich in sugar and condensed milk to recharge my depleted energy levels then joined forces with my mother-in-law to send me to bed while they looked after the baby. It was exactly what I needed and absolutely priceless.

So if you're wondering what to give a new parent for Christmas, give them the best gift of all: some sleep.

Soundtrack: 'Insomnia' - Faithless

BAGGY TROUSERS, DIRTY SHIRTS

I was surprised to receive an apology from a member of staff at my son's nursery a couple of weeks ago. Surprised because it was for something that I think is a normal part of childhood. The adults and children had been out in the gardens puddle-jumping and looking for worms which meant that I would need to put a set of the little man's clothes in the wash when I got home.

Checking that I hadn't mistakenly turned up at a Swiss finishing school, I told them that this was no problem at all. My son is a child and, like all children, he loves getting messy. Our washing machine is always on - my laundry basket literally runneth over - so this was no great shakes for me, but some parents had said they were not happy for their children's clothes to get dirty. Hence the apology.

I find this strange because being messy goes hand in hand with learning and growing. Some of the best photos we have of our children are of their first attempts to feed themselves: covered from nose to wrist in vividly-coloured purée, and beaming with pride at having (sort of) got the weaning spoon into their mouth. The pictures that we treasure are those first handprints and footprints created by chubby little palms and soles smeared with brightly coloured paint. The major event that is baby's 'first trip to the seaside' stays with you for at least a week as bits of sand continue to turn up in their hair/ears/nappy.

Then yesterday we were sorting through the children's clothes and my son put the three proper shirts that he owns on the 'too small' pile (they're not) and shouted "I don't like being smart!!" Much as I would love to see him just occasionally looking like a little Ralph Lauren model (in the vain hope that I might, by association, appear effortlessly chic and groomed) I thought he did have a point. He is happiest when comfortable, outside and preferably muddy. And I love him that way.

Soundtrack: 'Baggy Trousers' - Madness

PASS IT ON

Last year my husband and I sat down and told a (very professional and friendly) stranger our entire family and financial history and came away with a nicely presented set of instructions on what we would like to happen when we peg it. As unsettling as the process was, we congratulated ourselves on completing the grown-up task of having our wills written.

Then the other day, I was sat on the floor in the living room with my children. For once the television was off and we were playing snap. My daughter told me that she wanted to play a different card game and I remembered a game that my dad taught me: a version of patience called 'Beat the Clock'.

This is pretty much the only other card game I know - don't come calling for me if you need a Bridge partner - but as I set the cards out into their clock face and explained how the game worked I had a sense of passing something important on.

We played the game several times, holding our breath with each turn of a card that in the hope that a king wouldn't show up and congratulating ourselves each time a number on the clock was completed.

In the course of teaching this game to the children I realised that whilst there are no family heirlooms to connect the children to their granddad they now have 'his' card game.

We patted ourselves on the back for getting our wills written, but I gave myself a huge hug for giving our children a connection to the granddad they never knew. I hope they teach the game to their children.

WILD BOYS

I read an article in *The Times* a couple of weeks ago written by a mother of three boys explaining how she manages, in a house full of smelly sports kit and unpredictable explosions of energy, to maintain a sense of the feminine.

She gave advice on coping with the desires that most small boys have to own weaponry (or re-purpose items of furniture to represent swords and guns), eat constantly, and their need to be exercised twice daily much in the way that you would walk a dog. Forget a walk or a snack at your peril, for if your son is hungry or bored then your tidy living room is toast.

I checked this with a friend of mine who is also a mother to three 'blue ones' and she concurred that it is indeed a very particular experience when you are a parent to more than one boy (and especially if you only have boys).

For me, the article contained a massive 'aha' moment. In a 'light bulb going on' way, not in a 'being trapped in a cartoon à la Morten Harket' way. It read: "At around the age of four, boys experience a surge in testosterone which explains their obsession with characters and light sabres." So that's it! This is why our day begins with a running commentary on Spiderman, Batman, and whether Catwoman is a baddie or a goodie (in case you're wondering, she's a baddie).

This is why the only way we could stop our son from writhing around bellowing "NEVER!" in a muddy field, so aggrieved was he at being made to go for a walk, was to list all of the superheroes we could think of.

This is why there are two cutlasses in the boot of my car instead of an emergency blanket, torch, and spade. Ok, part of that is my fault for not buying the requisite 'dig-yourself-out-of-a-ditch-in-the-dark-whilst-maintaining-a-degree-of-warmth-using-some-tartan-wool' kit but the cutlasses are most definitely his.

And when we had his best friend over for the day it is why they practised flying kung fu kicks on the trampoline much to the distress of our daughter who was hoping for something a little less ‘fighty’. With the power of his buddy, we got to see our son in full-on masculine mode and wondered quite how the pre-school teachers manage ten boys on a daily basis all getting their testosterone groove on. However the teachers do it, we salute them.

Of course it wouldn't be me if I didn't make reference to equality for the girls in all of this. I wouldn't for a moment suggest they are the opposite of the above. Girls are of course shouty, ‘fighty’, active, funny, loving, and (just like their brothers) very hard work at times. We had one particularly incredible tantrum that involved our daughter blocking the doorway to Monsoon and I have thrown more than my fair share of toys out of my pram (and mobile phones across the room). But these boys, well, they're just a little bit more...wild.

Soundtrack: 'Wild Boys' – Duran Duran

WHAT WILL I BE?

On the way to a soft-play venue today (terrible weather = trip to a building made of tin filled with more scramble nets and obstacles than the finale of the Krypton Factor) the children were having a discussion with their cousins about what boys and girls are able to do. After five minutes on the merits, strengths, and abilities of girls and boys (including "girls can do sport if they are as strong as boys" and "I'm never getting married!"), it was agreed that actually they can do the same things, be it football, work, raising children, or the type of vehicle they fly/sail/drive. With the children's ages ranging between four and seven, I was impressed that they had raised a topic, debated it openly (and forcefully at times) then come to an agreement.

Given that it was a discussion between two girls and two boys, I was especially delighted that they came to the conclusion that they did. And then I remembered that children have an in-built sense of justice and fairness. Whether it's a board game, handing out sweets, portion-size at dinner time, or discussing who could be an astronaut, they each want to be treated the same and see it is only fair that others are too. What open-minded, smart, fantastic little people they are - I hope they carry this into their adult lives.

I am hopeful for this generation; they are the children for whom no stigma is attached to families where both parents pursue fulfilling careers, where mum has the more demanding/important job, or where dad stays at home to support mum's career. Whatever our opinions about family arrangements and career decisions that are different to our own, these children see them as normal. And in this I see that my son knows he can be an engineer, a teacher, a builder, a developer or a stay-at-home dad. And I see that my daughter knows she can be an engineer, a teacher, a builder, a developer or a stay-at-home mum. They can be anything, equally. Except as it stands today, some 'grown ups' have decided that girls cannot grow up to be a bishop in the Church of England. I think they could learn a thing or two from these kids.

Soundtrack: 'Que Sera Sera' - Doris Day

HI, MY NAME IS

What's in a name? Your parents pick one for you and you either love it, loathe it, change it, or your mates decide that adding a 'y' on the end of your surname or calling you something entirely different would work better. The latter point seems particularly prevalent among men. When I met my husband's friends I had to learn their actual names and their nicknames. Some followed the classic 'y' model – 'Broomy' and 'Studdy' being two such examples - whilst others stemmed from in-jokes and shenanigans long before I knew them – names like 'Queenie' and 'Shed'. This never happened with my girlfriends: our 'proper' names always won out.

So it was decided that I would be Toni, and whilst there have been a couple of attempts at variations from friends and the occasional syllable shortening to 'Tone' my name has remained largely unchanged and problem-free… except that:

- It is impossible for me to buy plane tickets or fill out a form without it being questioned.

- When I had short hair as a child, people thought that I was a boy.

- Sometimes, when my mother and father-in-law spoke to people about their son and me without explaining that I was a woman, some of them thought I was a man.

- Sometimes in business if I email someone prior to meeting them, they expect to meet a man (do you detect a pattern here?).

Were it to happen after a meeting, I would be distressed, but as that is not the case, the fact that my name creates confusion is something that I quite enjoy and so I thank my parents for giving me a memorable name.

So we skip through life with our first names then some of us become a 'Mrs' and change our surnames. Big day, big admin task, then big thrill of being addressed as Mrs Kent for the first time. So rarely do we use our formal names now, I feel like I'm in Downton Abbey if I have to say it or reply to it. It feels particularly strange to be called it by our daughter's classmates. Most of the time I don't feel too much older than 25 (even if I am much closer to 40) so it feels odd to be given such a respectable sounding title.

And so to those children. Ah lovely little babies that you are, we await your first word with trepidation, punch the air when you babble "mama" and are overwhelmed when you say mummy properly. Then you realise that saying mummy gets you attention, and the urgency and pitch with which it is delivered can be extremely effective in causing your parent to appear at a moment's notice. Uh-oh. Mummy becomes Muh-meeee.
Or Muuuuuuuuuuuummmmyyyyyyyyy. Or MummyMummyMummyMummy! There are days when I think that I must be called it close to 50 times...oh the agony. Sometimes it is cute, sometimes just about bearable, often absolutely maddening. There is a special kind of restraint involved to swallow the primordial scream brewing in your chest when you realise that the sound of you shutting the toilet door will prompt a small voice to call your name in a way that suggests something needs your immediate attention. Even an attempt to discreetly open a magazine at the kitchen table when you think your child is playing in another room gets picked up by their radar - how do they do it?

I love my children and being a mum has enriched my life but oh how I cherish those moments when I am just plain old Toni. Hang on a minute - I think I can hear someone calling from upstairs... no, I'm ok. This time it's Daaaaaaaadeeeeeeeee :).

Soundtrack: 'My Name Is'- Eminem

I BELIEVE IN FATHER CHRISTMAS

Belief is a funny thing, a personal thing, and one that is thrown into sharp relief at this time of year. Families that don't believe in God attend crib services and become teary-eyed on hearing 'Little Donkey', committed atheists can be cajoled into putting their bum on a freezing cold pew for Midnight Mass, and everyone over the age of twelve pretends for the sake of the little ones that a jolly man in a red suit zips around the world on a sleigh pulled by animals devoid of wings to deliver their presents. Factor in that our daughter lost a tooth two weeks before Christmas and we have had a festive season packed full of myth and make-believe.

Our most magical moment came this year when we put the children's letter to Father Christmas in the fireplace. Carefully written by our six-year-old and placed in the grate by our four-year-old, they mused on how it would reach Santa and whether we had left it too late (it was the week before, so they had a point). I don't know what distracted them but, for a moment, they looked away and by some incredible fluke, I managed to flick the envelope up the chimney where it caught on something and held fast (and still is – I must remember to get it out before it comes back down, it would rather give the game away or make them think he didn't want their letter and I'm not sure we have enough tissues to deal with the flood of tears that would cause). I managed to stand up before the children turned around to see the letter had gone, but couldn't quite arrange my features to disguise my surprise at overcoming my left-handed lack of co-ordination in such an impressive way. The look on their faces was priceless, and I think they took my open-mouth/raised eyebrows combo as confirmation that there was indeed magic afoot. Eat your heart out David Blaine!

I know at some point they're going to rumble us, and that we'll have to confess to the staging, secrecy, and hiding of presents in ever more hard-to-reach places but on the basis of that one reaction, we're going to keep it going for as long as we can. I wonder what the going rate is to hire a reindeer for next year?

Soundtrack: '*I Believe in Father Christmas*' - *Greg Lake*

7 LET'S GET PHYSICAL

Were it not for the mental and physical fix I get from running, it is entirely possible I would have spontaneously combusted by now. These are my tributes to putting one foot in front of the other.

HUMAN RACING

Today I took part in a race across nine kilometres of rain-soaked farmland. It's part of our annual village fête and attracts a range of people from casual runners to athletes in training for big events.

At the start I saw a neighbour who is one of those athletes: super fit and frequently first in the races she takes part in. We had a chat during the warm up and she said that regardless of her placing, her main focus was to enjoy it. It was exactly the pep-talk I needed to get into the mind set of finding fun in every sodden, boggy stride.

With the amount of club vests on display you could tell there were many people here trying to ace their personal best or secure a top three placing, but twice during the run, I saw people stop to check up on fellow club members who had slowed or looked like they were in trouble. Friendship had taken priority over finish time.

Eight kilometres gone with a hill climbed and a field of maize crossed in my waterlogged trainers (it was like being in a low-budget horror film - running through waist-high crops with the sound of someone else's footsteps and heavy breathing behind you) a lady began to keep pace with me. We ran together for most of the last kilometre, keeping each other going, as by that point we were both bright red in the face and the tired legs feeling had well and truly kicked in. In the last two hundred metres, she put her hand on my shoulder and said "go on, off you go" - she knew I'd seen my children which had given me the extra boost required to sprint for the finish.

I spoke to her afterwards to say thank you, and to my surprised she thanked me for giving her a pace to aim for -

she had been following me from the start. It was great to think that in a race I had entered on my own, someone had been running 'with' me the whole way.

During the time that it had taken me to complete the run I had seen in this competition kindness, compassion, friendship and acknowledgement of your fellow man. It was truly a 'Human Race'.

PS: If you're wondering about my neighbour who took time out of her warm-up to motivate me, she did (of course) finish first!

Soundtrack: 'Human Racing' – Nik Kershaw

LET'S GO OUTSIDE

On moving to the Newbury countryside eight years ago, and being a staunch advocate of punishing classes at large gyms, I wondered how on earth I was going to stay fit now that I lived many miles from a David Lloyd facility.

For the first six months, I thought that a really smart and not at all unsociable thing to do would be to leave the house at 6am to get to a 7am class. This meant missing breakfast with my husband and any opportunity to use a decent hairdryer but hey, at least I will have had an hour with a man wearing boxing pads shouting at me to "hit them harder you wuss!" to get my day off to a nice mellow start.

Eventually I came to realise that this was an expensive and quite frankly mad way to keep fit. The tipping point was an incident where I managed to forget my work clothes and had to drive into Reading to buy something to wear for my 9.30 meeting. As laid back as my boss was, I think even he would have drawn the line at sweat-soaked lycra as appropriate business attire. So I raced into town, and by 8.45 was hopping from foot to foot outside M&S looking very dishevelled and with the mad stare of a woman waiting for the Harrods sale. Despite me trying to smile nicely and explain my predicament to the shop assistant as she opened the doors, she became very pre-occupied with getting as far away from me as possible. This was understandable, given the circumstances.

After the embarrassment and expense of that workout, I cancelled the membership and looked for an alternative way to keep fit. At the weekend we often rode our bikes along the Ridgeway and it struck me that with a bit of diary reorganisation I could swap the gym for the countryside and ever since have been enjoying the benefits of outdoor exercise. I knew it was as good for your mental well-being as for your physical well-being, but hadn't anticipated these added extras:

– There is never anyone else's sweat on your bike seat and you will never find yourself having your workout interrupted by a woman in a day-glo unitard saying "Aren't you finished on that bike yet? I need it."

– You never have to run/cycle in front of a screen specialising in music videos of men in t-shirts the size of dresses surrounded by greased up women in strips of elastic tempting them with their 'jelly'.

– You don't have to listen to people roaring/huffing/accidentally dropping their guts through the effort of lifting weights the size of a family car.

– You might see a horse but not a man in shorts that are too tight (hopefully).

– You might smell manure but you won't smell someone else's BO.

– It's free and always open.

So I am sold on outdoor exercise but brilliant as this is, will concede there are times when you need a bit of coaching and motivation. The solution lay in a conversation with a neighbour: turns out she also wanted a bit of fresh air and exercise so now we are running buddies which means that not only are we getting the benefit of the great outdoors, but we're building a friendship too.

Soundtrack: 'Outside' – George Michael

I WANT TO RUN

Oh running, where would I be without you? This morning I was greeted by a beautiful frost-fringed scene and pure clean air. For someone who loves the combination of this kind of weather and a canter through the countryside, it was like catnip to me: I did the school run and then went for a run.

For most of us our first encounter with running is an enforced cross-country trek in t-shirt and shorts while being barked at by your PE teacher and prevented from dawdling by another teacher at the rear. For me this meant a red-faced, stinging-thighed, chest-flapping experience. As we were more concerned about fashion than correct sportswear, we wore plimsolls instead of good trainers, Top Shop bra-tops instead of sports bras and character t-shirts instead of anything that would keep us vaguely warm. It was a terrible combination and not something that inspired many of us to carry on.

But carry on (and off) I did. I joined the local athletics club and after coming last in every race I was entered into, I was put in the walking race. That's right – the walking race! Where you must walk fast, but not run, forcing you to waddle like a Pearly King with his thumbs in his braces dancing to 'My Old Man's a Dustman'. It is a terrible look, a terrible sport, and I came second to last because someone else had to pull out due to injury. Not a natural sportswoman but not to be undeterred by this lack of prowess in the competitive arena, I decided to try to keep fit with a friend who, like me, mistook her teenage curves to be lard, by running with bin liners under our t-shirts like boxers did. We didn't develop six-packs, we just got sweaty. And rustly. We looked and sounded silly, so we stopped.

I decided from there on in to stick to the gym, generally going at silly-o-clock in the morning for an hour with an ex-Army PT instructor who had decided what he really wanted to do was shout at out-of-shape office workers. And then my mum had heart failure and I thought I'd give running another go by signing up to do the Reading Half Marathon, partly to raise money for the British Heart Foundation, partly to help counterbalance the amount of curry and beer I was enjoying at the time, and partly to hopefully reduce the chances of it happening to me. There is nothing like the prospect of having to run 13.1 miles to force you out into the elements with (very importantly) the right footwear and undergarments. Once I'd run my first mile without having to stop I was hooked. I don't think I'd quite appreciated how good it would feel.

That's not to say it doesn't have its drawbacks: I've lost toenails, got lost, fallen over, fallen into a bog whilst trying to guess a route through some woods next to the Kennet and Avon canal, had to run with the equivalent of a snail trail on my running tights after spitting on myself (I know it's not very nice but I now understand why footballers are always flobbing), been bitten on the backside by a dog called Billy, had upset stomachs, headaches, and farted in front of a fellow runner - hard to hold in a trouser cough when in motion (apologies but sometimes your body just doesn't 'do' polite). I've developed blisters, chilblains, almost fainted from dehydration and am now addicted to glucosamine to try to combat the clicking noise that my hips make but I will keep doing it because I've found nothing that beats the mind-clearing, freedom-bringing, good to be alive feeling that comes from a nice long run. Think I might go for another run tomorrow...

Soundtrack: 'Where the Streets Have No Name' - U2

8 TECHNO

Sometimes I marvel at technology. But most of the time I just want to poke it in its virtual eyes.

WHERE IS MY MIND?

There was a time when the amount of email received in a day was paraded as the mark of a true warrior. Ok, not the mark of a true warrior, more the mark of someone who thinks that being sent loads of stuff makes them look very important. I will confess to having been involved in conversations with colleagues where we compared the volume of messages received and nodded gravely in agreement at how very busy we were. Strange stuff. You would never brag about the amount of post that you get through your letter box or the amount of conversations that you have. Can you imagine saying: "You'll never believe it, I got home to find seven letters on the doormat and that was after I'd spoken to at least twelve people on the phone and met precisely five more. Really, the amount of communication I've had to take part in today has made me feel incredibly weary."? No, you would sound like an idiot. So why is it different when it's digital?

I have a long history with email, from managing the single account belonging to my workplace many moons ago to running three separate accounts today. I would struggle to get by without it, and I do like it when it's properly used. I have also experienced the thrill of receiving a company-wide email with the title "Please delete the previous email immediately" which of course means that everyone reads it, saves it, and its contents become more interesting and explosive than the latest episode of whatever soap nobody watches together these days. It has had its moments.

But here's the thing... Somewhere along the line I had forgotten that I can choose what email I receive and respond to and my email accounts were filling up with sales messages that I didn't want. Every day yielded a digital disappointment as I would miss a message from my friend in Australia because it was lost in a sea of 'SHOP NOW' emails from companies I don't want to hear from. No, Wallpaper Direct, I have no desire to do another eight weeks of decorating this year, thank you very much.

The same goes for Facebook status updates and LinkedIn discussion threads that drip into my accounts by the minute. If I'm not 'there' then I can't properly contribute, and these endless blips and updating inboxes are distracting me from the stuff I should be doing and smothering the messages I should be seeing (like those from my accountant - sorry!) which makes me feel annoyingly disorganised. No wonder people frown when they look at their phones. I blame mine for the irritatingly wonky lines that are forming between my eyebrows.

Of course you could apply lots of lovely rules, sweeps and automatic clean-ups but this makes you keep shed loads of unwanted mail 'just in case'. You wouldn't keep every pizza flyer or double-glazing leaflet or save every voicemail you received so why store every email? Unfortunately, as our email accounts are not like the cupboard under the stairs which will eventually burst forth if you shove even one more toy in it, we end up with years of dusty, pointless old data and I have had enough.

There's nothing for it but to be ruthless. I'm going on a mission to remove all the rubbish and ditch the endless offers from Debenhams (sorry Debenhams but there's only so many Blue Cross Sales a girl can take) after which I shall clap my hands over my computer and chime Indian bells to get my digital chakras in order. I'm going to detox the inbox.

Soundtrack: 'Where Is My Mind' - Pixies

YOU DOWN WITH OPP?

Despite a career in tech I'm still a laggard when it comes to all things computing. It wasn't until 2011 that I joined Facebook and predictably it is now one of my favourite things for keeping in touch with friends and family. Scratch that, it's probably my favourite way of keeping in touch with almost everyone apart from a good face-to-face chat. Preferably with wine involved (and there's plenty of that on Facebook - by 5pm on a Friday every status I see involves having, or wishing to have a drink).

I knew on joining Facebook there would be friends that post their every waking moment, those that dip in and out and those that are rarely there. They might not be there at the same time or for the same reason but the thing they all do is post photos. Endless photos. Photos of birthdays, holidays, 'we went to the park' days. They document christenings, Christmas, 'Christ I was a drunk-mess'. The ability to share so much of your life with so many people without looking like a crazy-lady showing off the family album at a bus stop (even if it isn't too far removed) is a most tantalising thing.

What I hadn't anticipated was to be on Facebook, you have to be ok with Other People's Pets (you see, not the OPP you might have been thinking of you naughties!) The amount of pet-based posting that goes on initially stunned me. There's reams of it. Streams of it. Pages and pages dedicated to it. There isn't a moment when my timeline doesn't have a photo or comment about someone's puppy or kitten. And if it isn't their own they're posting a link to a photo or video of an animal that has amused them. At this very moment I can see an image of Robert Downey Jnr's head on a cat's body... Unexpected, and of niche appeal but it's there and I have seen it. And now, so can you.

Some friends' profile pictures have morphed into pictures of their pets and in one instance my friend's pet has her own page. Her own page AND 31 FRIENDS! If ever proof were needed that the British are soft about animals, this is a classic case in point and I rather like it. But I did feel a bit left out.

We had come to the conclusion that we would be a 'pet free' family after being scarred by the experience of a cat that made regular and vigorous dirty protests after our children were born (it turns out she was more of a 'prefers to be fussed by a kindly old lady' than 'kept on high alert by children' feline). Our village has more puppies than pushchairs so whether I am at the school gate or online, I am never more than a minute away from a loopy Labrador or a charming King Charles but we resolved to stay firm; our house is not ready for a pup that will eat its way through our furniture. Even if they do look at you with adoring eyes or give you a level of obedience that your children never will, we are not getting a dog. Yet.

But we have caved in, just a little bit. Because children don't forget when you make them a promise years before that you will bring something small and fluffy into the house for them to love. So now a corner of our garden is given over to four very funny, slightly naughty, fabulous egg-producing hens. Within the space of two hours, I had gone from "meh" to "mine" and...posted their picture on Facebook.

As unimportant as it no doubt is, there are times when it feels vital to observe an animal to improve the quality of your day. I hope I can now return the favour to my friends who have lifted my spirits with pictures of their furry-faced companions… even if they do have Robert Downey Jnr's face superimposed on them...

PS If you're interested to know quite how important animals are to the Internet age, might I suggest you head to YouTube to search for and watch 'The Internet is Made of Cats' by Rather Good Stuff.

Soundtrack: 'O.P.P.' - Naughty by Nature - definitely not about pets.

FOR YOUR EYES ONLY

Hands up who owns *'Fifty Shades of Grey'*? You do? You naughty monkeys!

But how many of you would happily leave it lying around the house within sight of the children / the in-laws / the new friend you've just made through the school run?

For years, people have been disguising their reading matter, from the man hiding a 'specialist magazine' within a newspaper to adult Harry Potter fans concealing the original cover. In the latter instance the publishers had the idea of producing a more grown-up sleeve but by and large if you didn't want people to know what you were reading you had to hide it.

And then the Kindle came along and we didn't have to do this anymore. We can travel to work reading something subversive or sit in Costa consuming something rude with our latte. Far easier to casually slip a Kindle out of sight or turn off its screen than try to force a 533-page copy of 'Mrs Spanky's Midnight Visitor' into your handbag before the person next to you sees it.

As a lover of books I was unsure that an e-reader would be for me; there's nothing quite like the look and feel of a book, and to receive one as a gift shows that someone has really thought about you (unless perhaps you're a woman who has been bought Ian Botham's autobiography, or a pensioner who's been bought a Viz annual). I think it's important to have books within reach of our children to encourage them to read frequently and widely and hopefully instil a passion for language. That said, the advent of our daughter learning to read means that some books have had to be moved up high. And if I have to climb on a chair to reach them, they're not getting read.

With the introduction of a Kindle into our house I can now have whatever reading matter I choose without fear of it being stumbled upon by the children and my handbag is considerably lighter. Sold to the lady who likes sweary fiction.

I thought that these were the two main benefits until I spoke to a friend who lives in the UAE. She told me that 'Fifty Shades..' is banned in her country and whilst there was not the option of picking it up at the local bookshop she had been able to download it onto her Kindle. It's not a revolutionary read, and hardly an important read, but right there was an act of civil disobedience - go Mrs! I hadn't before considered the power of an e-reader to put content into the hands of people who otherwise might not be able to access it, whether that's due to a government wanting to keep information from its citizens or being too old or infirm to leave your house.

So despite the well-reasoned arguments against them, I am all for e-readers for their ability to give more people access to more books, for helping to make sure my children don't end up learning lots of swear words because I've left Frankie Boyle's latest book lying around, and for making saucy stories written for women more mainstream. Which reminds me: there's a bit of reading I need to catch up on...

Soundtrack: For Your Eyes Only – Sheena Easton

IF I HAD A PHOTOGRAPH OF YOU

There are 586 photos on my phone. Not content with managing calls, appointments and emails the phone has stealthily become my camera. On the PC, there are thousands of pictures. In the photo albums there are a couple of hundred, and 15 have made it onto our walls; a wedding photo, baby faces and a first day at school all captured for posterity.

Most of the pictures are of the children. A colleague wisely predicted that the birth of our first child would coincide with the purchase of a new camera as well as the mountain of baby-related goodies you actually need. He was, of course, correct.

Of the first 10 years of my life, there are about 30 photos. Perhaps because there are so few, each of them seems to carry a huge amount of sentiment and capture a special moment in time. It has made me wonder what will become of the endless shots that we take of our children: stored on hard drives, SD cards and SIM cards, sometimes shown, but rarely printed. When they get older, will the children want to see them or will they even be able to find them? Will we ever be able to encourage our children to sit still for long enough for them to even begin to look through the hundreds, if not thousands of images that exist of them?

What the children do seem to really enjoy though is going through the albums where they can touch the pictures and take them out for closer inspection. 'Getting the photos out' is something that they find quite exciting - particularly when they get to see pictures like the one of me dressed proudly in my Brownie uniform as my brother stood bare-chested next to me taking the mickey out of my pose. I was so pleased to be joining the Brownies that I wanted my first day recorded for posterity - they prefer their uncle's stance.

This has spurred me on to sort through all of the digital photos, get the important ones printed and delete the duplicates. I'm also resolving to spend more time in the moment with them, rather than trying to document their every move. If I was, or wanted to be, a great photographer it would be different, but what I'm aiming for is to be a better parent so I'm putting the camera, and the phone, down.

Soundtrack: 'Wishing (If I Had a Photograph of You)' – A Flock of Seagulls

I CAN SEE CLEARLY NOW

From my 'Because You're Worth it' post you might think that I would shy away from having a bit of work done to my face but that is not strictly true.

A few years ago I was woken in the night by a great deal of crashing and banging coming from the kitchen. Concerned that the noise would wake our sleeping baby (and given she was a baby that didn't go in for sleeping at night very often I definitely did not want her to wake up), I decided to go downstairs and find out what the source of the noise was.

On reaching the kitchen I discovered that it was being created by our cat, Phoebe. She was streaking across the room, leaping from table to worktop, her back legs skidding and knocking everything within reach onto the floor before she finished with a flea-like leap to the top of the cupboards. My soothing calls for her to come down succeeded only in her hurling herself towards me. She glanced my elbow, skimmed across the kitchen floor then threw herself up the stairs and into the bathroom where the crashing of pans turned into the thumping of shampoo bottles hitting the deck.

By this point, my husband had woken up and followed me to the bathroom to find out what the hell was going on. I explained the situation and he switched the light on to reveal Phoebe balancing precariously on the shower. He took one look and said, "Toni, that's not our cat" before heading downstairs to get a broom to usher the invading feline out of our house. The thing was, you see, is that I was very short-sighted without my glasses and so mistook the aggressive, long-jumping mad cat for our passive, timid, lazy puss on the basis that they had vaguely the same black and white markings. It was then I decided to get my eyes lasered and a couple of years later, I finally gathered up the cash and the courage to do it.

Much as having your eyelids held apart à la A Clockwork Orange is an unpleasant sensation (especially having it done after you've seen the film), and having to put eye drops in every day for eight weeks is a faff, the results are astonishing. Within a couple of days the world had gone all HD on me and, for the first week or two, I was in complete awe at the detail I could see. It does wear off a little when you realise that you also get to enjoy crystal clear rendering of other people's nasal hair and dandruff but even so, I am still amazed with, and delighted by, what eight minutes of lasering can achieve.

It's something that I've recommended to friends and, as my husband is short-sighted, we did discuss the potential for him to have it done. He's decided against it but that's not such a bad thing as I've realised it that when he takes his glasses off, it doesn't matter if I've not plucked and buffed myself to within an inch of my life: he sees me in soft focus – result!

Soundtrack: 'I Can See Clearly Now' - Jimmy Cliff

TECHNO, TECHNO, TECHNO, TECH-NO!

We are preparing to embark on our first holiday abroad with the children. It's just a short hop to Spain but with the associated travelling to and from airports we're potentially looking at a six to seven hour journey door-to-door.

A journey of this length (or in fact any journey in our case) means that the children need to be entertained. Six to seven hours is a long time to keep children quiet and happy but outside of the unavoidable screens on the aeroplane, I don't intend to give them a piece of technology to do it.

I didn't get an iPod until about four years ago (and, of course, immediately wondered how I ever lived without it) and no longer have satnav in the car but I am very much a tech-lover. The launch of the Microsoft Surface excites me, I am teetering on buying an iPad purely for the 'Paper' app, and I couldn't get through the day without my smartphone. As a freelancer I can't not be connected to email when I need it and I love keeping in touch with people on Facebook and Twitter but this does not extend to wanting to put gadgets into the hands of my children.

Of course we have a television, and of course the children are allowed to watch it but I would prefer that the majority of the gormless gazing at screens and furrowing of brows is left to the grown-ups in our house. There is an impressive but annoyingly wonky line that has developed between my eyebrows thanks to this and I am frequently told by the children to "stop looking at your phone!" And I think that's the way it should be. It's right that they should think distractedly looking at a screen when you should be paying attention to the people in the same room as you is wrong.

That's not to say the children don't access technology outside of our home. The most depressing thing I read in our son's otherwise brilliant pre-school report was that he had good mouse control. I couldn't give a monkey's uncle whether he can power up a PC, work a mouse, manipulate a touch screen or pull the back off a server; I'd have been happier if they'd told me he can make a farting noise by sticking his hand under his armpit. It is probably less than 5% of the time he spends doing other outdoor, physical, interactive, educational, fun stuff but it does make me a little bit sad that it is believed that children have to have some form of computer skills when they're not even old enough to write their own names.

Wow - that feels better, are you still here? Yes? Good. Thank you for listening.

So, back to the journey. How on earth are we going to cope? We're relying on good old-fashioned pens, colouring books, Top Trumps, and in a nice twist; a card-based version of Angry Birds. And if that doesn't work, we'll be conducting a mass singalong on the plane. Wish our fellow passengers good luck!

Soundtrack: 'No Limit' - 2 Unlimited

9 CULTURE CLUB

In my dream world I am a bohemian who holds impromptu poetry slams and makes amazing sculptures out of found items before popping round to see the Queens of the Stone Age for a jamming session. Meanwhile, back in the real world……

MUSIC IS MY RADAR

As you'll know from the majority of my post titles, music is a big part of my life and, like a lot of people, I can categorise certain parts of it by the music that I was listening to at the time.

My musical journey started as a child where my parents weaned us on The Jam, the Steve Miller Band and Blondie. I wanted to 'be like David Watts' and look like Debbie Harry. Other early highlights include singing 'I Feel Like I'm in Love' by Kelly Marie at primary school whilst doing a handstand, and when 'Hey Mickey' was released by Toni Basil I was thrilled that there was a (somewhat) famous female singer called Toni. See - it's not just a boy's name!

In my very early teenage years I forgot all the cool music that my parents had shared with me and my brothers and dived headlong into an obsessive attachment to Duran Duran (yes, I did practise signing my name as 'Toni Le Bon') who were then ditched in favour of Bros. I am now distanced far enough from those years to confess to wearing Grolsch bottle tops on my shoes to signify that I was a 'Brosette'. What the hell was that all about? Did Matt, Luke and Craig have some really lean years where they couldn't afford laces and had to make do with bottle tops to hold their shoes together? They were singularly responsible for our local pub putting up a sign to say they most certainly would not be giving them to children… not unless you looked over 18 and were prepared to pay for a bottle - as our friend's sister did. Result!

By the time that I had worked the "when I grow up I want to marry Simon Le Bon" phase out of my system and started using appropriate devices to keep my shoes on my feet, along came indie and how my tastes changed. My school books went from being decorated with love hearts to being covered in lyrics from The Wonder Stuff and the Happy Mondays and my Clarks school shoes and smart jumper were switched for monkey boots and a very tatty cardigan. I felt like a right rebel, and I looked like a right jumble sale.

After that, there followed brushes with heavy metal (I wanted to look like any of the women from Heart and almost got knocked out at an Acid Reign gig), swingbeat and RnB (I wanted to look like Louise Nurding and thought that the lyrics of R Kelly and Bell Biv DeVoe were romantic, until I learned that they are, in effect, a smooth way of saying "oh baby, please get yer knickers off or else I'll shag your best friend") and then on to hip hop which gave me the twin adolescent joys of dancing and expressing my anger at adults. My connection to this music never completely faded, as evidenced by a room full of white, middle class IT workers in black tie dancing to 'Get Low' by Flow Rida at a Microsoft conference in Washington three years ago. At the time it felt GREAT! To anyone watching it was probably SH...AMEFUL!

From hip hop I moved on to rock and then dance music. These last two genres have been my steadfast companions right up to today and I could bore you with tales of bad fashion, raves, gigs, and house parties but the point is that music was, and is, always there for me when I want to celebrate, commiserate, forget, remember or just let off a bit of steam. I remember our wedding reception as a series of songs, our children were born to music (and a bit of screaming, but I prefer to remember listening to 'Asleep in the Back' by Elbow playing on the titchy CD player in the delivery room...) and if ever there's a chance to leap around in a vaguely rhythmical fashion I'm on it, be it in the kitchen or at a ceilidh.

So, when tonight my six-year-old daughter returned from her school disco, beaming, rosy-cheeked, and stating "my feet hurt from all the dancing", it made my day. She's at the start of her musical journey, and I hope it will be as joyful and interesting as mine (but without the house parties - definitely no house parties).

Soundtrack: 'Music Is My Radar' - Blur

HIP HOP JUNKIE

Ah Basingstoke in the late '80s and early '90s: a shimmering new town full of hope, opportunity, and potential. Ok, maybe not that. A grey town centre populated by pigeons, a few punks still hanging on in there, and a writhing mass of teenagers wondering how the hell they were going to avoid marrying the boy with the limp / the girl with the wonky eyes, and living next door to their parents. We worked as cleaners, skived as much school as possible, used fake ID to get into the glory that was 'Martines' (a nightclub under a car park - woohoo!) and busted moves on sticky dance floors. It was also hip hop heaven.

Given that pretty much every house on the estates on which we lived had either a satellite dish or a 'Squarial' (remember those?) our televisual choices when it came to music changed from seeing Spandau Ballet on 'Top of the Pops' to being able to watch 24 hours solid of MTV and how we embraced it. 'Yo MTV Raps' gave me hip hop history as well as a shopping list for the next time I ventured into London to buy a black leather medallion from Camden market or something on import from Tower Records. We danced badly, wished we had porches on which we could 'hang-out', memorised lyrics and watched 'Boyz N the Hood' with the same intensity that we had watched 'The Breakfast Club' five years earlier.

Maybe it was the teenage desire to mark ourselves out as different and shock our parents but we embraced the stories told by these films and the words of the songs as if they were our own despite the fact that we lived closer to Guildford than we did to a ghetto.

I remember being engaged in a lengthy conversation with a man from the council who had come to fix our radiators and had taken exception on seeing my record collection. He decided to give me a long, racist, lecture which culminated in him suggesting that I wouldn't turn out to be any good if I carried on listening to black music. He had a point in that some of the language is not to everyone's taste and I would agree that some artists do not promote healthy attitudes towards women (2Live Crew anyone?) but music "turning you into a loser"? I don't think so. Hip hop and rap music did not turn me into a misogynistic, gun-toting, police-hating, welfare-reliant, potty-mouthed hoodlum. Quite the opposite. It gave me a medium to channel some of my adolescent fury, a way to indulge my love of language and to revel in fast-paced lyrical gymnastics. It made me think about how words affect other people and through albums like '3 Feet High and Rising' brought me a great deal of joy. It also meant that after leaving Microsoft, one of my first paid pieces of work was to write a rap for the Marketing Division of Progress Software. So thank you hip hop: you gave me the skills to pay the bills.

Soundtrack: 'Hip Hop Junkie' by Nice & Smooth

ART FOR ART'S SAKE

There is a scene in Crete that haunts me. It calls me, beckons me to immerse myself in its azure water then lie amongst the olive trees and doze under its hot, hot sun. But this isn't coming from across the sea - oh no. It's coming from my glorified shed. This scene is actually the subject of a painting that I should have finished by now, months and months in the making. Applying layers of colour then waiting for the oils to dry, then painting again. It gets left to wait whilst work, family, writing and a hundred other things jump the queue. Every now and then I imagine that the painting is annoyed and shouting at me so I go back to the shed and paint furiously for an hour and a little progress is made, but if I wait for a tidal wave of free time or an explosion of inspiration, it may never be completed.

I love to paint, love it. I painted lots in previous years. I sold a few paintings, gifted a few, donated a few but it takes a lot of time, peace and quiet that is very rare in our house these days so I am tempted away from my first love by the immediacy of writing. But I shall now use the power of writing to publicly kick my own arse into finishing this piece so the very understanding and extremely patient buyers can finally look out onto their little piece of Almirida, Kalyves and Chania, and I can then paint the pictures that will stop the bare walls of our living room from staring accusingly at me every time I go in there.

I know that painting won't be a career for me just yet. Given my work rate and our children's need to be shod on what seems like a six-weekly basis, both me and my husband need 'proper' jobs right now, but what I am committing to is getting back in that shed and finishing what I started, for the love of it, for the joy of it, for the making-someone-else-happy of it, for art's sake.

Soundtrack: 'Art for Arts Sake' by 10cc

This post was inspired by finding out that someone I worked with nearly twenty years ago, when we were both freight-forwarding chimps, is actually a fantastically talented artist. You can check out Robert *Fitzmaurice's work at http://robertfitzmaurice.co.uk*

Since the publication of the original blog post, the painting has actually been finished! You can view it at https://www.facebook.com/ArtbyToniKent

I'LL BE YOUR KARAOKE QUEEN

Pre-children, the main reason for raising my voice would be to get attention when five-deep at the bar in a nightclub, trying vainly to order a bottle of Becks by waving a ten pound note and shouting "Excuse me!"

When I raise my voice now, it's to encourage the children to do the thing I've asked them to do twenty-three times before. 'Super Nanny' states that you should never make a request more than twice - but I'm not having that and neither are the children. It has become a sport in our house to see how many times I have to ask before anything gets done. Occasionally, we'll have good family sing-a-long in the kitchen and I love to sing in the car but always with the windows firmly shut.

So it was with much trepidation that I agreed to participate in a karaoke evening. Of course these have been going for donkey's years and I am no stranger to singing to my heart's content at a gig or in the car but on this occasion there were lots of people there who regularly perform on stage and know how to carry a tune or two. That, and the fact the music was provided by a pianist, made me rather nervous, but I had promised myself that I would sing, and sing I did.

In perusing the list of songs, which included show tunes, pop, classic duets and a bit of rock thrown in for good measure, I didn't think about where my vocal range might best be suited and instead plumped for a song that I like and know most of the words to: 'I Predict a Riot' by the Kaiser Chiefs.

In the car, I sound amazing. Through speakers, with just a piano for accompaniment, in a small pub, is quite a different matter. The pianist was game though, nodding encouragement and helping out on the la-la-la-la la-laaas that come before the chorus. At the end he said that I "had acted in the true spirit of karaoke" by which I think he meant, 'it was a bit shit but you it gave your best'.

Afterwards my friend was very kind, offering congratulations as another singer gave a frankly jaw dropping rendition of Born to be Wild. My pride was somewhat saved by a drunk couple who each sang a song dedicated to the other. She looked lovingly at him and sang Eternal Flame. By way of response he sang angrily at her that "your sex is on fire!" - and they say that romance is dead..

That evening my heart had pounded so hard it felt like it would burst out of my chest and all I had done was sing a song aloud in public, at an event specifically designed for that purpose. And because it made me feel that way, so nervous and excited, I think I'm going to do it again, but next time I'll pick a safer song.

Soundtrack: 'Karaoke Queen' - Catatonia

10 GOOD, GOOD PEOPLE

As well as collecting words I also collect experiences and memories of being with, near or inspired by people who prove that the world has not, as the Daily Mail would have us believe, 'gone to the dogs'. Here are a few of those smart, funny, generous people (and one hell of a rock god).

YOU CAN SAY WHAT YOU WANT

On Thursday night I went to the Cosmo Blog Awards in London to find out if I had won in the Next sponsored 'Best Newcomer' category. From thousands of entries I was shortlisted as one of the final 15 and, suitably excited and dressed up, I headed to London Town.

The evening started with me walking into the Three Tuns, a pub around the corner from the venue (the Rose Club on Orchard Street, in case you're interested). It was heaving with people having post-work drinks, slaking their thirst before the journey home or settling in for an evening of sherbets and shenanigans. There is something about going into a pub in London at 5.30pm that to me is very thrilling, in a way that the same drinks in say, Reading or Slough would not be, can't think why. Anyway, amongst all the suits I spotted two ladies who looked from their outfits like they were headed to the same place as me, so I grabbed a beer, wandered over to them and said "hi".

Luckily for me I was right. They were two lovely fellow bloggers, Miss Budget Beauty and Dolce Vanity. We formed a trio, hung out for the evening and when Dolce Vanity was announced as the winner in the Best Established Beauty Blog category, it was fantastic to celebrate with her. As it turned out she was the only one of the three of us to walk away with a prize, but I had a great night and tottered home with a goodie bag that was chock-full of rather nice things.

I met lots of new people, made some good connections, and have since spent some time reading a few more of the shortlisted blogs as well as catching up on some old favourites. The range of topics is incredible with some people sharing pretty much every waking moment of their lives and others specialising in one field. What really stands out in their writing is not product reviews, fashion tips or best cupcake (oh when are we going to be free of the damn things!) recipes, but when they speak from the heart about things that are important to them. I have read moving accounts about mental health, hilarious posts on childbirth and passionate pleas for us to be kinder to one another. It's not all ultra-earnest either. One of my favourite blogs is from a shepherd who runs team building events built around herding sheep *(www.teambuildingwithsheep.co.uk)*.

Pretty much every one of these bloggers feels free to write about whatever they like - something I only felt confident to do after becoming a freelancer and something I wish I'd started sooner. Former colleagues have said to me they've a whole list of things they can't do until they're 'free' and what a shame this is.

I know so many interesting, funny, smart people and a whole host of them are locking this part of themselves away but until when? There are books, poems and posts unwritten, ideas for podcasts, and paintings that never make it onto a canvas. Someone I spoke to recently about publishing options told me that the most interesting thing about me had been I used to work for Microsoft (oh dear) but (thankfully) it is now my writing that counts.

I am very proud of my career but don't want it to be my defining quality, how sad would it be to be remembered only for the company you work for? So if you have got a writer within or an artist hiding away in your heart - don't keep them trapped under a corporate bushel - let them out!

Soundtrack: 'Say What You Want' - Texas

GOT MY ORANGE CRUSH

With Bradley Wiggins' triumphant addition of another Olympic gold to his medal tally, being the first Brit to win the Tour De France under his belt, and exceeding Sir Steve Redgrave's medal haul to become Britain's most decorated Olympian (an accolade he shares with Chris Hoy since this was first published) I thought now would be a good time to extol the virtues of 'the redhead'.

Being born with bright orange hair, I was adored and indulged by my Irish grandmother (what is it with elderly Irish ladies? They love a ginger-haired baby!), and called 'Goldilocks' by my mum who would brush my hair until it shone. Less charitably I was called 'ginger nut' at primary school. Disappointingly, this still happens among adults - what gives?

The red wasn't destined to stay and I went from orange to ginger to strawberry blonde to whatever number it is on the colour chart that my hairdresser uses but I still get excited to see a redhead give their childhood bullies the equivalent of a big v-sign by being successful.

A case in point was a recent 'Wiggo' post-Olympic photoshoot. Not content with being superhuman, he managed to rock sitting on a golden throne with his kit unzipped to the navel whilst giving a peace sign. Only the truly outstanding among us can carry that look off.

Aside from this Titian titan, here are some of my other favourite redheads:

Daniel Craig - finally a Bond to give the girls a run for their money in the swimsuit department.

Karen Elson - born in Britain, massive in America, stunningly gorgeous model and super cool singer.

Nicole Kidman - smart enough to ditch Tom Cruise early on.

Josh Homme - Queens of the Stone Age frontman, amazing 'axe'-wielder, friend of Dave Grohl and very fine looking indeed.

Ronald Bilius Weasley - funny, magical and he gets the girl. *In your face* Potter!

Nicola Roberts of Girls Aloud - not content with being part of one of the biggest girl bands of all time; she got serious, became celebrated within broadsheets and high fashion magazines, and her public stance on the damage caused by sunbeds helped to get a bill passed which banned them from use by under-18s. Hats off to that woman!

I'd also like to acknowledge a few lesser-known redheads in my immediate circle of family and friends: Vicki, who was building a successful online business before most of us had figured out text messaging; Laura, of the band Fairfolk who has a voice as mellifluous as her hair is vibrant; Lucy, who wore a Monroe-style wedding gown with more sophistication and class than a blonde ever could; Auntie Karen, who was my first example of an 'independent woman'; and my niece Leila, who at the age of four is already proving to be a talented actress.

So here's to Bradley Wiggins: so cool that Paul Weller thinks he's cool. The man's a legend and a ginger. Judging by all the spectators wearing ginger 'lamb chop' sideburns at the Olympics, I can feel a trend towards people asking for red the next time they visit the salon - the future's orange.

Soundtrack: 'Orange Crush' – R.E.M.

I AM ONLY 24 HOURS FROM…

Within my group of friends, colleagues and family are people with an incredible array of skills and professions. I know teachers, roofers, a journalist, photographers and producers. I know small business owners and Corporate Vice Presidents, mothers of five who work, and stay-at-home fathers. I know someone who has acted at the Edinburgh Fringe, mum's with degrees in Japanese and mathematics and dyslexic people who didn't excel at school but have gone on to be hugely successful in business.

And where their skills and career choices may differ wildly, they all have at least one thing in common: Just 24 hours in a day and a choice on what to do with that time.

This thought was prompted by an email I received a few weeks ago via LinkedIn that casually informed me that one of my friends had a new job: he's now a Clinical Scientist.

I got in touch to say congratulations and express my delight that I now know a scientist. His reply was, "Thanks, it only took ten years of studying and a further ten years at work to get there...."

I started thinking about how other friends had got to where they are. The ones who followed their calling into journalism, photography, and production did not 'fall into' their jobs. I remember the years of them being skint and slogging their guts out at the bottom of their professions. The Corporate VP works until 11pm, and often later, every night because she's driven by wanting to be able to offer her children every possible opportunity. My brother can take me on a tour of the houses that are watertight because he spent years on building sites learning how to put up roofs. Then there are those that volunteer hours of their time to pre-schools, Scout groups and charities because they want to pass on skills for life, motivate children and directly improve the lives of others. These are focused people who have put in years of effort because they have a clear picture of where they want to get to and what they want to achieve.

So I will follow their examples and make sure that I am dedicating proper time to what I want to achieve; their success reminds me that you only get out what you put in. And because I do not want my epitaph to be: "She was never published because she kept watching repeats of My Big Fat Gypsy Wedding", you will now find me writing in the evening and not in front of the TV...

Soundtrack: 'Twenty Four Hours From Tulsa' – Gene Pitney

WHO YOU GONNA CALL?

When I was 18, I packed my belongings into my auntie's car (she of the 'Got my Orange Crush' post) and she transported me a couple of miles away to where I was to rent a room in a big house. Oh the freedom, the excitement, the 'being skint' because all of my wages went on rent and the train fare to Reading. Due to a combination of the wrong location and an odd landlord, my choice of first home was pants, and walking two miles to ask my mum for baked beans because I'd run out of money was a joke, so I decided that I would move to the town that is almost a city: Reading. (You've got to admire the optimism of a council that decrees the buses shall say 'city' in the belief that one day the Queen will bestow that honour).

Anyhow, to Reading I went and if I thought that living in a rented room two miles from home was bad then living twenty-five miles away was, in some regards, worse. I had more money but I was now a long way from my family and the friends that I had grown up with. I didn't bump into people I knew anymore, we didn't have mobile phones, and so, as often happens, we started to lose touch. I regularly went back 'home' for full-on weekends of merriment but that made the weeks feel even more lonely. It was during that period that I realised that making truly good friends (you know, the ones you can call at 2am through a haze of tears and snot and they won't disown you), takes a lot of time and shared history.

Happily I stuck it out, more of those friendships came (and still endure), and it's because of that move that I met my husband so I have much to thank my teenage determination for. It also meant that I came to value those good friendships even more.

What is interesting to me now is how this works when you are a parent without those strong friendships in place . For us and many of the parents at my daughter's school, this village is the second or third place we've lived, so lots of us are away from the network of friends and family we may have enjoyed if we'd stayed where we were born. What was so lovely when my daughter started school was that within the first term, phone numbers were exchanged in case anyone needed a hand in an emergency. We all knew how stressful things could become when you're trying to run a family, manage your career and make an attempt at a social life. We all understood that mornings do not run smoothly and that the A34 is a magnet for jack-knifed lorries that prevent us from making pick-up. We all appreciated that not everyone is able to make time for sports day / harvest festival / assembly. I have been the person to take the, "Sh*t! I'm stuck in a 12-mile traffic jam, can you collect my children please?" call, and I have been the person that has made it.

Whether deepest, closest friends or not much more than acquaintances, everyone is up for helping each other out at a moment's notice when it comes to the children and that has an incredibly positive impact on everyone's experience of having children at school. There are no tallies to be kept or expected favours, it's just how the village works. As long as we remember the right number to call when drunk and emotional and feeling like we need someone to talk to...

Soundtrack: 'Ghostbusters' - Ray Parker Jr.

YOU CAN GET IT IF YOU REALLY WANT

For the past two Monday nights, I have found myself sat in a very welcoming kitchen with excellent company. Some of us know each other well, some of us only met last Monday but we each have the same thing in common; one beautiful friend*.

For those of you that read the blog post dedicated to her, you will know that last year, our beautiful friend helped to arrange some events for our village. The Easter one was so successful that the local tourist information office called one of the girls to ask if it was happening again this year. It was only ever intended to be a one-off but the call sparked an idea to hold it again as a tribute to her, raising funds for the local cancer charities that so helped her and her family.

The only slight snag is that from phone call to event we have but three weeks. We are almost two weeks in and it has been frankly incredible what a small group of people with access to some technology and a network of extremely generous local people can achieve.

So far, between us we have managed to source the most eclectic array of goods since Del Boy closed the doors to his lock-up. We have:

One venue, six gazebos, three banners and dozens of posters, three chickens, a lamb, two hundred eggs, an unspecified number of rabbits (well you know what they're like for breeding..), face paints, raffle prizes, a PA system, one 'tug-o-war' rope…*At this point would you mind if I indulged myself to bellow "FIVE GOLD RINGS"?.....*

We also have:

Vintage china, a coconut shy, the commitment of the entire Key Stage 1 of the local school to produce Easter bonnets, one tractor and two ponies. Phew!

And, should disaster strike due to the wonderful British weather, we've even got a backup plan thanks to the kindness of our local Scout troop.

Everything we have been able to acquire at little, or no cost which means the charities receive more, and everybody gets a little bit of something that money can't buy: the pleasure that comes with giving something out of kindness.

The levels of generosity, understanding, willingness to help, good humour and teamwork has been good for the soul and will result in something that hopefully will do our friend, and her family proud. Who knows what the next Monday meeting will bring and who knows how the event will work out but what we do know is that we'll do it just as she would have done: with laughter, positivity, and by the seat of our pants!

Soundtrack: 'You Can Get It If You Really Want' – Jimmy Cliff

** Read 'My Beautiful Friend' at the end of this book.*

SCOUTING FOR GIRLS

At the age of 16, a friend and I boarded a train to a nearby village to go to a party. So preoccupied had we been with securing cans of Special Brew and menthol cigarettes (sophisticated or what?), we didn't give a second thought to how, or indeed if, we were going to get home. There was always the prospect of a friend's floor, or in the worst case, calling my mate's dad to come and collect us.

I will spare you the full details of the evening but needless to say we ended up drunk, deserted by friends, and with no idea of where we were going to sleep. After a brief discussion we agreed that calling home to ask for a lift was out of the question. We had, of course, lied about where we were and 2am is never a good time to call your dad in a drunken stupor and announce you are in need of a lift home for the third time in a month. Please.

We instead returned to the train station where we had earlier alighted and found it to be deserted and freezing. As you can't 'plump up' a wooden bench, sleep was not forthcoming so we ended up in a dilapidated hut that offered a bit more shelter and set about building a fire. The only problem was that we had nothing suitable to build a fire with, and, as both of us came from families that were very light on the whole 'outdoors experience', we didn't have the nous to fashion something a la Bear Grylls.

What we tried to do was start a fire using the only thing we had that we thought was flammable: a box of Tampax. To that we added some printed materials which we found near the hut. In the dark we did not know what they were. Under the light of our matches, we saw that they were a pictorial study in the anatomy of women and wished we had never touched them.

We discovered that night that tampons are not good fire-lighters and that you should never go scavenging for stuff to start a fire with if you don't have a torch, lest you should encounter some 'specialist' magazines. You live and learn...

So what's this got to do with anything? Well, the point of it is that my daughter has recently joined the first group within the Scouting family: Beaver Scouts. As a former Brownie and Guide (girls were not permitted to join Scouts back then), I didn't know what to expect. One term in and she has already taken part in archery, a woodland exploration that involved leaping in a huge bog, following a line blindfolded and building a shelter, and - most recently - building a fire. These are girls and boys between the age of six and eight who, far from being cosseted and wrapped up in cotton wool, are being given freedom, the opportunity to try new things, learn useful skills and succeed in all sorts of different areas. Best of all, they are having an absolute ball.

As a result I'm sold on it and wish that I'd had the chance to join the Scouts. I'm not sure whether it would have stopped me from going to the party, but I sure as hell would have been able to light that fire!

THERE GOES MY HERO

I am watching one of my favourite bands - The Foo Fighters - perform at the Reading Festival. Unfortunately this post is not coming from the festival itself, but my living room...something that I plan to rectify next year.

Seeing Dave Grohl in action is a particularly life-affirming experience as he manages to combine raw power, musical genius and the biggest grin in rock to deliver a masterclass in connecting with an audience. As they've been going for nearly twenty years the Foo Fighters' music has soundtracked my adult life and the last time I saw them live I had to be dragged from the moshpit due to nearly passing out. The reason? I was (unknown to me) two weeks pregnant and my body was not pleased at the weekend of drinking and leaping around I was trying to inflict upon it.

Apart from my attachment to their music what really does it for me is watching someone doing something that they so obviously love. There's this guy, creating a brilliant thing to share with other people and having the time of his bloody life doing it. You can't fake that kind of passion and energy and it's made me realise why I'm so attached to the experience - I want a piece of that!

Before you become too alarmed I am not about to embark on a singing career but what Mr Grohl has just provided me with is a motivational boost to pursue my writing career with even more gusto. Participating in a satisfactory business meeting will not make me feel like a rock star but getting published will.

So here's to all the people that are already rocking out in their day to day lives, turning what they love into their career - I look forward to joining you soon!

Soundtrack: 'My Hero' – Foo Fighters

11 LEFTFIELD

It's the second to last chapter and what do I have for you? A little bit of left-handedness, proof that country life is anything but boring, a moustache story and musings on whether Iain Duncan-Smith really thought about what it might be like to live on next to nothing before stating that he would if he had to…

LEFTISM

I am at secondary school. We are on the top playground, being taught tennis.

Mr Knight, resplendent in maroon nylon tracksuit - just a single white stripe on the sleeves, no super-fly Adidas breakdancing tracksuit for him - is alternately encouraging, then berating the class.

We are instructed to hold the racket in our right hand, lift it high, then throw the ball up with our left hand to serve. Mr Knight looks at the lines of children facing each other across the nets and realises that the picture he is seeing is not as pleasingly symmetrical as it should be. A pause, and then:

"And for the cack-handers, *THIS* is how you do it!"

And so it continued. Rounders, cricket, hockey. One set of instructions delivered normally, then a second set of instructions that began with taking the piss out of the left-handed children.

To be fair to him, I didn't take offence then, and I don't now. Of all our teachers, he was probably one of the most fun to be taught by, and probably because he did so much stress-busting exercise that the experience of teaching thirty largely disruptive, uninterested, kids did not leave him feeling like he was having a nervous breakdown, and us feeling like we were a wrong answer away from being beaten to death with his Dunlops.

I'm left-handed and proud and very much enjoy the fact that in some cases it unnerves people. Left-handers are folks to be suspicious of. Just look at them with their hands concealing their writing, what are they writing about? This is amplified by the use of mind-mapping. A left-hander taking notes in the form of a diagram? Burn the witch!

Approximately ten years ago I was part of a management team that consisted of three left-handed people. When the next person to join the team was similarly 'blessed', fellow colleagues suspected we were planning a coup. If only it were that exciting. We were actually trying to decide how best to manage the merger of two businesses acquired by Microsoft in the UK (how exciting!) and so carried on writing our plans on a white-board. Plans that would enable the business to make progress and leave us with the 'mark of the leftie' because we could wield neither marker nor ink pen without creating a dirty great smear down the side of our left hand. We forged ahead whilst the rest of the business considered throwing us into the lake at Thames Valley Park to see if we would float.

There are a quite a few things, particularly in the sporting arena, I can't do well that may well be down to being a southpaw, but could just as well be down to lack of practice or inclination. I am also a bit of liability when it comes to sharp knives and meal preparation (see 'Oliver's Army' for more on that) but fortunately my husband is a right-handed kitchen magician so we eat well and rarely visit A&E. There are, however, some areas where I am more dextrous than some of my right-handed cousins. And husband.

I can paint, sketch, draw, write a story as tall as you like, and tie a bow tie (more frequently needed than you might think), and when I went to give blood on Friday, whilst the vein in my right arm was not up to the job, the one in my left arm was declared to be "Marvellous! Twice the size of the other!" Half a litre delivered in ten minutes - boom! I may be crap at mixed-doubles and useless at rounders, but I can create, and entertain, and give to others, so that's alright by me.

So next time you meet a left-handed person, don't run in the opposite direction, or suspect foul play if they're writing notes, or laugh at their inability to hold a tennis racket. Shake them by the hand. But not the left hand. That would just be weird.

Soundtrack: 'Leftism' – Leftfield

DOWN IN THE COUNTRY

Ah the countryside. Peace and quiet, pipe and slippers, an absence of street lights and a sky full of stars. Idyllic and boring as hell by turns. Or is it?

I grew up in Basingstoke: a town that gets a very bad rap but actually has some nice countryside on its doorstep. Walks to the local farm were commonplace, as was being told off by the farm manager for touching the electric fence 'for a laugh'.

From there to Reading for a ten year feast of pubs, clubs, restaurants, and shopping. Happy, happy, days but there came the point when the paper-thin walls of our Victorian terraced house (we knew our neighbours far better than we wanted to, or perhaps they intended us to - rather like my friend in 'Summer Loving') and spending an hour stuck in traffic to travel eight miles lost its shine, so we departed to a village in the Berkshire countryside.

It ticks all of the boxes you would expect: horses on the high street, tractors on the school run, sheep and cows coming up to the garden fence and visitors from nearby towns wandering the streets searching in vain for a mobile signal. If you don't have a car, you are at the mercy of just six buses a day and if you are sick, you had better make it between the hours of 9 and 12 if you want to be seen at the local surgery. So far, so predictable, except that lots of far from predictable things have happened in the eight years that we've been here:

– The bike ride where we encountered a full-blown rave happening in an underpass.

– The pig running purposefully up the road en route to

who knows where but certainly escaping being turned into chops.

- The 'Missing Llama' poster that appeared in our shop window.

- The naked rambler who wasn't quick enough with his modesty screen to escape a friend's husband from seeing his rambling buttocks winking in the sun.

- The house that keeps a flock of rheas in its garden.

- The weather being something of real interest rather than something that just happens outside. Snow closes the village off. Torrential rain brings a normally dry river back to life and sends shoals of 'Monster' energy drink cans through the village (other heart palpitation inducing beverages are available). It also threw our trampoline across the garden with the gusto of a fast-bowler.

- Discovering the best way to break into your house after locking yourself out is with the help of a heavily pregnant woman and a 12-foot ladder.

- Bumping into people we last saw in the moshpit at the Reading Festival at a Scout meeting.

- Being told that a pub in a nearby village was to be avoided due to the feistiness of the local jockeys and stable hands. Oh how I wished to see silks flying but we heeded the warning and relied on our imagination to fill in the blanks.

So eight years in, we're looking forward to at least eight years more and for a move that we thought was all about space, and peace and quiet, it has instead been one of discovery, amusement, and surprises. Ravers, llamas, and naked ramblers - not so boring after all.

Soundtrack: 'In the Country' - Cliff Richard and The Shadows

GET INTO THE GROOVE

With January nearly at a close I had hoped to be more organised by now, settled fully into the new year with clear plans for the next eleven months.

We painfully ground through the gears of dragging ourselves out of our Christmas cocoon and into the first weeks back at school, pre-school, work and, in my case, starting a new job. By now, we should have made a clear transition from a boundary-free festive season (see 'How Soon is Now') to clearly planned, precision-timed, actions and activities. But no, not us.

My son caught norovirus, and two days later so did I. And then it snowed so much that the village school had to shut, so my husband and I worked from home and took it in turns to pull our daughter around on a sledge. Then we had a weekend of pulling both of our children around on their sledges which was actually great fun because we caught up with friends and found our tricep muscles. And then school reopened but our daughter caught a virus which kept her off for three days. Fortunately, it was nothing serious, so after a sigh of relief I allowed myself a strangulated, "Aargh!"

Aiming to get back into the groove after Christmas has felt like trying to tidy up during a children's party: very hard work and ultimately fruitless and frustrating. A bit like a dog chasing its tail.

But come Friday, it will be February and I will try again, and who knows, perhaps I'll catch my tail by the end of the month!

Soundtrack: 'Into The Groove' - Madonna

YOU WANT TO LIVE LIKE COMMON PEOPLE?

As further cuts came into force through the government's Welfare Reform Act 2012, Iain Duncan Smith said, "I could live on £53 a week if I had to." A petition has been set up to see if he would like to prove it, but of course he could live on £53 'if he had to'. We all could, because in a situation where you have no choice, where you have little income and are reliant on the state to support you to some extent, or totally, then you just get on with it. Many families already do.

This is not about to become a tirade against people who rely on benefits, nor a lengthy defence. What it is about is requesting a little more understanding of how bloody hard it can be to work your way out of that situation.

When I was growing up, both of my parents had low-paid jobs. Dad got home from work in the late afternoon and was immediately handed the parenting baton so mum could go to work in the evening at a shampoo factory. Our family was dual-income but we had bugger all to show for it. No holidays, just hand-me-downs and great smelling hair - thanks Alberto Balsam! We did, however, have an appreciation of the importance of work because during the short periods when my dad didn't have a job, it massively impacted our household budget. This was to become permanent however due to his ill health and subsequent death. Without the benefits system as it was in the late 80's/ early 90's, I have absolutely no idea how my family would have survived.

When you are poor and a teenager, and wishing that your dad wasn't dead, and that you had enough money to get the bus and not have to walk three miles to town, and that you didn't have to wash your clothes in the sink because the washing machine is broken, and that you didn't have to keep asking the neighbours for bread and sugar, and all the other stuff that goes along with living on almost nothing and everybody knowing about it, you are in quite a precarious position. You really are only a couple of choices away from being reliant on benefits for the rest of your life. But if you can see through the grief and the shame and the sick and tired feeling that comes from relying on hand-outs, that it is possible to get out of this kind of situation, it might light a fire underneath you that makes you work like a bitch to do everything you can to get out. Which is what I did.

And because I saw that possibility, and went after it like a girl possessed, I know how hard it is to move away from home at eighteen with nothing to fall back on, to leave behind friends, family and siblings that need you. I know what it feels like to spend 90% of your wages on rent and train fare meaning you have to live off beans and marmite sandwiches for most meals (not together of course, that would just be wrong). I understand the difficulty in making friends when you've moved to a place where you don't know anybody, the feeling of being out-of-place, lacking confidence, not having the right social skills and struggling to shut away the part of you that thinks you don't belong. I know what it's like to rent a room in a house that seems fine then the landlord turns out to be very weird indeed so you don't feel safe and you end up jamming your bedroom door shut by putting a chair under the handle. It is far, far easier to not do this stuff, to 'stay put' where you feel more comfortable, and are among the people you grew up with.

But I'm so glad I didn't go back because every minute of effort was worth it to reach the evening in the Bull &

Chequers when I was introduced to the man that is now my husband. That is not to downplay the fantastic friends I have made and the career I have enjoyed. Lots of great stuff has happened and overall things have worked out well - my teenage self would be jumping for joy at the life I now have - but his support has changed my life and so without him it wouldn't mean quite so much. And, of course, had we not met, we wouldn't have had our children, little smashers that they are. So thanks 'the B&C', I owe you one.

So far, so very lovely and heart-warming, see kids - getting 'on your bike' works! But my point is this. Finding the strength to invest that kind of effort and cope with the moments of loneliness, 'being broke-ness', and generally feeling like you're dragging Eric Pickles uphill on a sledge is just about do-able when you're young, single, healthy, positive to the point of naivety and have a couple of A-levels. But to find yourself in that position in your forties, with a family, or because your partner has died, or because you are ill, or if, for whatever reason, you came out of school with no qualifications. How much harder is it then?

The government wants people less reliant on benefits and more inclined to work and yes, I agree. There is pride and fulfilment in going to work, bringing home a wage and feeling that you have made a contribution. It gives you confidence when you have your own money and feel in control of your circumstances. It feels incredible to achieve things in our professional and personal lives but what if something happens that takes those things away or knocks you so far back that you wonder how you'll recover? Could you just 'snap out of it' then?

So yes Iain, help people to make changes, find a way to bring more work into families and make more choices available to young people who aren't starting out from a solid foundation. But do it with a little more understanding and perspective and don't think that platitudes like yours work when delivered by someone earning over £130,000 a year. We could all live off £53 a week if we had to, but we sure as hell wouldn't choose to.

Soundtrack: 'Common People' - Pulp

HOW 'MO' CAN YOU GO?

There is a moustache or 'Mo' growing in my house. Not quite 'salt and pepper', but definitely more than a hint of grey going on within the black, it is a blatant and bristly intruder. The children complain of its itchiness when they kiss Daddy goodnight and I try not to stare in incredulity at the changed face of my husband, but we know that it is there for a good cause and so we wait patiently for December to arrive when normal service will be resumed and kisses will be smooth once again, all the while being grateful that the 'Mo' is there to support, rather than to remember.

I love the creativity and participation that Movember encourages, the way it tackles a serious issue in a positive way and the variety of spin-offs that it has created, from MoRunning, to the individual efforts of people who will recreate a moustachioed pose of your choosing every week, subject to a donation to prostate cancer charities.

I know that this topic, and this month, is much documented and so I didn't think I would have anything different or interesting to add until I came across a condom company that is run by a friend of a friend. One of their recent Facebook posts carried a picture that manages to combine sexual health and Movember in a way that some people thought was a bit close to the edge but I found very salutary and funny. After giving it some thought I have decided not to publish the picture because I'd like to give you the choice as to whether you look at it or not, but I think you will be able to imagine it when I tell you that the gentleman's rather full and lustrous moustache does not belong to him, rather it is the pubic hair of a woman. It is well-shot, humourous rather than sexual, and supportive of women in that I think it is possibly the first instance I've seen where a company is using an image of a woman with full pubic hair in a positive way. If you would like to take a look - you'll find it at www.facebook.com/safesexappeal.

Whether you check out (or agree with) the picture or not, I hope that you will join me in celebrating Movember. Whether you 'grow a Mo', run for miles, splurge on sponsorship or simply acknowledge the facial hair efforts your friends and neighbours make in the name of cancer awareness and prevention – we can all play a part!

*Soundtrack: Born to Hand Jive - Sha-Na-Na (*from *Grease: The Original Soundtrack from the Motion Picture)*

12 TIME TO SAY GOODBYE

The final chapter, containing a single post dedicated to someone that lived her life with an energy and joy that few ever achieve. She's still shining bright in the lives of everyone who was lucky enough to meet her.

MY BEAUTIFUL FRIEND

I dreamed about you again last night. We are laughing; you are funny, smiling, alive. And then I wake up and realise in the darkness of the room that the reason I dream of you is because you are gone.

We haven't been friends for that long in the grand scheme of things. Not for us the 'in-jokes' of the playground, shared youth, or drunken teenage holidays. We are grown-ups, mothers, when we meet for the first time.

You live at the end of my road and yet the first time we say hello is when I recognise your car outside the nursery five miles away. The little white Audi with a company number plate. As we talk our boys grab one another and laugh and we realise that they are the ones that the other is always talking about. They are buddies. 'Little Learners' in nursery parlance and completely loony in each other's company.

And once we've met each other for the first time, we seem to see each other all the time. I am admiring your vintage-style engagement ring and you tell me about your New Year's Eve wedding plans.

Then you're back from your honeymoon and we're talking again and swapping stories of our shared wish to escape our corporate lives and you cheer me on so I take the plunge and you're not far behind. We drink tea in your kitchen out of bone china cups that are not 'crazed' because you know how to spot a good one and this becomes the strength of your business and soon you are hiring out china to the BA Concorde Lounge for the Queen's Jubilee and I am excited that you've bagged a big one and you are laughing at the strangeness of it all.

Then I'm trying to figure out Twitter and you sit down and teach me because you were taught by a friend who is a dentist and we laugh that I'm from IT and yet bloody clueless about this thing and then I walk you through LinkedIn and we are evens, but you have the nicer teeth and can refer me to your friend.

And then there's the party between Christmas and New Year when you introduce me and my husband to your friends and you welcome us with champagne, then feed us red wine and cheese that your dad has sent to you, and the cheese doesn't work as a means to prevent drunkenness and then we are bellowing out Rod Stewart songs and the children are embarrassed and my husband has to look after us all (including my son who shut his finger in a door) and I forget my handbag and have to sheepishly return to reclaim it. And I am mortified but you are generous enough to say, "It's not a problem, we were all a bit pissed."

And there's more tea and garden centre lunches and visits to soft play where our boys race around until they sweat and their hair smells so good and their cheeks flush as if slapped. They are Spiderman and Superman, Lightning McQueen and Mater, Thor and Captain America. We drink overpriced coffee and don't mind the expense as our boys are exhausted and we've had time to chat.

You join a team of great women to walk the Moonwalk and arrange events for the village that raise huge sums of money and at no point do you say "poor me" because you have had cancer.

Then I'm out for a run and a Porsche whips round the corner and I see you before you see me because I have run these country roads for years and know to keep the volume on my iPod way down low so I can hear the roar of an engine and you go home and tell your husband that I was "bloody running towards you" and he agrees I was on the right side of the road but mental to be on that windy stretch.

And we go to a barn dance and you're both using a Welsh accent and making me double-up with laughter because you're singing a Goldie Lookin Chain song and my friend thinks you're actually Welsh, and the barn dance ends too soon so we buy more wine and head back to yours and before I know it, you're both walking me the two hundred metres home just to make sure I get back ok, and in the morning my husband wants to know why there's a broken wine glass in the bin. It's your 'one for the road'.

We talk about school and the handful our boys will be together. It snows and snows, and our husbands are pulling the boys up the lane on sledges. We are side by side in your kitchen of vintage china and family photographs and you talk about your husband and how you are glad he is here with his son and can 'do these kinds of things'. You take photos and videos and borrow my wellies which is a mistake because a foot out of the door means you're fair game and a snowball is shoved down your back.

For a week your boy rides with mine to pre-school and every morning you kiss him goodbye with both hands clasped to his face and tell him you love him. And you say "thank you" when you don't need to and take the time to match your headscarf to the rest of your outfit and we drink ludicrously strong coffee that makes my head swim. And the last time I see you we don't hug but embrace.

And we knew it might come but it happened so quickly, we are stopped in mid-sentence, my beautiful friend.

This is dedicated to the beautiful Belinda Harding-Perry.

ABOUT THE AUTHOR

Toni Kent was born and brought up in Basingstoke. She had an 'interesting' time at school which she left at the age of 16 in order to search for employment and riches. After a false start in a fruit and veg shop where she was frequently badgered by old ladies about why baking potatoes were priced 'each' rather than 'per pound' she decided that maybe education did have its uses and went to college, after which she joined the corporate circus.

All was going swimmingly until her children informed her she'd turned into Robot Mummy: woman of high heels, short fuse and stony face so at the age of thirty-six she harnessed her long past teenage rebellion, stuck her tongue out at 'The Man', and gave up the car, pension and endless lattes to become a freelance writer.

Thanks to the insight and intervention of her children, Toni now spends her time writing copy for businesses, stories for primary school children, and her blog 'Reasons to be Cheerful' which you can read at www.tonikent.blogspot.co.uk. This is her first book.

ABOUT THE ARTIST

The cover art for Reasons to be Cheerful, Part One was created by the artist Tony Cocks, who lives in London with his wife and their two Hungarian Vizslas (aka the 'Ginger Ninjas'). When not combining his dual passions of Lego and Star Wars to create stunning artworks he retreats to a studio where he records the odd voiceover and history podcast. He finds time fit in a day job talking about technology. A man of few words but many talents, he describes himself as follows: Geekish. Podcaster. Photographer. Voiceover artist. Apprentice Polymath. Mitchell Bros stunt double.

Tony's artwork can be found on the walls of some rather fine establishments and at www.bingethinkingphotography.com

Made in the USA
Charleston, SC
31 January 2016